Contents

Introduction 02
Getting Ready 03
- *Printing surfaces* 03
- *Tools & materials* 05
- *Overview of cloth & media* 05

The Thermofax Screen 07
- *What is it?* 07
- *Advantages & disadvantages* 07
- *Suitable Imagery* 08
- *Burning the mesh & making the screen* 12

Using the Thermofax Screen 16
- *Overview of media* 16
- *Developing good technique* 17
- *Clean-up* 21
- *Design adjustments & repairs* 23

Projects; exploring ways forward 25
- *A note on composition* 25
- *Layering values* 26
- *Layering colour(s)* 27
- *Line into texture* 30
- *Layering scale* 30
- *Soy wax resist* 31
- *Freezer paper stencils & resists* 32
- *Exploring transparency & opacity* 33
- *Working with sheers* 33

Media & Recipes 37
- *Soda soaking* 38
- *Chemical water* 39
- *Print paste* 39
- *Making dye paints* 40
- *Batching & rinsing* 41
- *Discharge paste* 42
- *Fabric paints & acrylics* 44
- *Soy Wax* 45

Colour Mixing 47
Resources/Suppliers 52
Further Reading 54
About Committed to Cloth 55

Detail of 'Stormy Skies' by Sarah Welsby

Introduction

We were introduced to the thermofax screen many years ago by Jane Dunnewold, and immediately recognised it's potential as an alternative to photo-emulsion designs on a traditional silkscreen. At that time, our studio facilities didn't have room for the production of photo-emulsion screens, so thermofax screens became our tool of choice when it came to generating fine-line imagery.

In simple terms, a thermofax screen is a small, imaged silkscreen. It's light-weight, takes up little storage space, is easy to use and easy to make – or have made for you - but more on that in the main body of the book.

Whilst we've published a book on creative ways of getting a design on to a traditional silkscreen, there are times when you want the kind of imagery that only a thermofax or photo emulsion screen can give you. The power of the thermofax lies in its capability to print very fine line designs; handwriting, a spider's web, old documents such as birth certificates or school reports, sketches and so forth.

Some people think that acquiring a thermofax screen means owning the machine that will burn the image for you. This isn't necessary as there are many companies who will provide this service – all you need to do is provide the imagery and they do the rest – for a fee of course! You'll find such suppliers listed in the Resources section at the back of the book.

This book has been written to help you explore the potential of the thermofax screen in terms of bringing your personal imagery alive. We suggest you sit comfortably and read the book through from cover to cover. Take a look at the pictures, be inspired and then make a decision as to where to start – which could be anywhere.

Enjoy the process, and enjoy being in a creative space.

Detail of 'Bewegung' (Movement) by Claudia Helmer

Getting Ready

Before we look at the thermofax in detail, it makes sense to cover the preparation you'll need to undertake to get ready for printing. Having done that, we'll then get stuck in to how to make and use a thermofax screen.

The approaches in this book enable you to use a variety of different media. Some are messier than others but if you don't have a studio, a little organisation and planning mean you can work in the kitchen, in the dining room, the garden shed, the garage or even a shady spot in the garden.

Whilst the thermofax screen tends to be less messy than some other approaches, it's still important to set up the work space. If possible, use an area with washable surfaces, or lay down a decorator's cloth or a couple of old sheets you can wash and re-use. Worrying about drips and spills will tighten you up. You'll also need somewhere to wash the screen and the squeegee. For most thermofax screens, the kitchen sink will be big enough, and a reasonable alternative is a large plastic box parked outside near a drain, filled with water from a hose. Place the box on a small picnic table so you don't have to bend.

Printing Surfaces / Workbenches

If you have to bend too much when painting or printing your back will complain. Ideally, you want the top of your table to be at the height of your pubic bone; about kitchen worktop height – between 85-95cm/40" – 42" – depending on how tall you are. Consider raising your kitchen table on bricks, wooden blocks or pipes. We use plastic plumbers' pipe with a thick piece of wood stuffed inside. The wooden bung is cut to the length the table needs to be raised, then jammed into one end of the wooden pipe. The table legs then slot into the other end of the pipe and sit on the bung, raising the table accordingly.

Our print boards/tables are made from either 9 or 12mm (1/2") MDF or Plywood that can be cut to any size. When considering size, if you're using a kitchen or the garden as a temporary studio, make sure you can lift the board on to a table by yourself. If you're creating a dedicated space/studio, make a print board as large as the space will allow; you'll never regret having a decent-sized work surface to play on.

Cover the plywood with two layers of acrylic or craft felt – stretched and stapled to secure it. Two layers of old blanket or even a layer of old-fashioned carpet underlay/padding is also a good option but either way, avoid a consistency that's too soft/spongy. The print board can be stored behind a wardrobe, under a bed or in the garage/shed – so with a bit of effort, any area can be turned into a studio for a day.

For most of our wet processes we cover the print board with a drop cloth; heavy cotton drill/broadcloth are good options as they're nice and thick and last for ages. The job of the drop cloth is to absorb excess wet media, prevent bleeding and protect your felt covering from becoming damp and contaminated with media. Some of ours have become so magnificent they've been withdrawn from service and turned into storage bags for our work.

Lightweight table risers made from plumbing pipe and wooden bungs

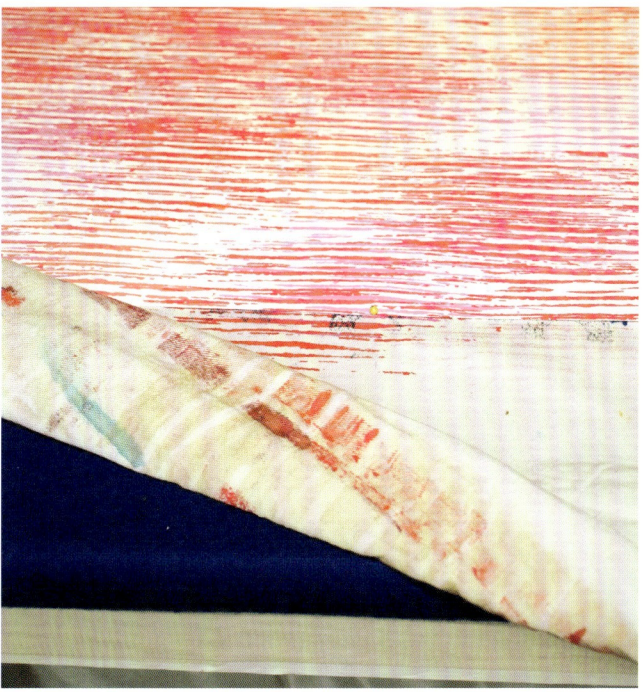

A print table covered with two layers of acrylic felt and a drop cloth

TOOLS & MATERIALS

As this is a book about the creative use of the thermofax screen, the list of requirements is relatively short! You will need:

Tools:
- Thermofax screens in imagery of your choice, made to the appropriate size.
- A couple of squeegees; traditional squeegees (such as the 9" Speedball variety) tend to be too large and too aggressive for use with a thermofax. Some suppliers have sourced and sell suitable thermofax squeegees but a good option is a small grouting squeegee/spreader that can be found in most DIY/hardware or kitchen stores. At worst, you can use an old credit card. We've also tested other ways of pushing the media through the imaged mesh, but more on that later.

Materials/equipment: the materials you'll need will easily fit into a plastic storage box.

- A printing surface, covered with the drop cloth, as described on page 3
- A lidded plastic container for storing print paste (the size will depend on how much you make)
- A bucket for mixing chemical water, and a lidded container to store it in (plastic water bottles are fine)
- 6 to 10 old spoons (we prefer metal to plastic)
- Measuring spoons (teaspoons and tablespoons are the key measures)
- A measuring jug
- 2 metres/yards of sturdy sheet plastic
- Plastic containers for storing thickened dye paints or discharge paste; squeeze bottles are very convenient – we use old ketchup bottles or sauce bottles bought from a catering supplies company.
- Some small pots for colour mixing; old yoghurt pots will work fine.
- Masking tape
- Kitchen towel
- A box of ball-headed or T pins
- Freezer paper (optional)
- Soy wax and associated tools (optional)
- Washable P.V.A. glue (optional)

We cover the different types of media in more detail on pages 37 to 45, but essentially, you'll be able to use the following:

- Cloth that's appropriate for the media you're going to use (see notes on page 37).
- Procion-type Mx fibre-reactive dye in a personal selection of colours.
- Chemical Water ingredients (recipe provided on page 39): Urea, water softener and Resist Salt L/Ludigol.
- Additive for print paste: sodium alginate (Manutex RS). Recipe provided on page 39.
- Jacquard discharge paste or Formosol powder/crystals for making your own discharge paste (recipe provided on page 42).
- Fabric paints and transparent extender base (information provided on page 44).

The Cloth
We provide more detailed information on fabric choices on page 37, but felt it would be helpful to provide an overview here.

The type of cloth you use will depend on the chosen media, for example:

- *Fibre-reactive Mx thickened dye paints;* Mx dye paints are suitable for all natural fibres except wool.
- *Discharge paste;* will discharge Mx dyed cloth, with the exception of Turquoise which is usually resistant to discharge processes. Commercially dyed black discharge fabric should work, but always test a sample first.
- *Fabric paints;* fabric paints and acrylics will work on any fibre – including synthetics - as they sit on the surface of the cloth and have no chemical reaction to it.
- *Washable P.V.A. glue (school glue);* this can be printed on as a resist when using thickened dyes.

Washing/Scouring the Cloth
Generally speaking, it's best to scour your cloth before using it. Whilst some cloth is supplied 'PFD' (meaning it's prepared for dyeing), others may not, particularly if bought from retailers or market stalls etc. Scouring removes the size or dressing on the cloth that will prevent dye paints and discharge paste from penetrating the fibres.

To guarantee removal of size, it helps to scour fabric in a rinsing agent such as Synthrapol SP/Metapex 38 and soda ash/sodium carbonate. Textile rinsing agents are designed to remove size from fabric or catch up, hold and remove excess dye from fabric. For scouring with a rinsing agent and Soda Ash, follow the instructions on page 37.

A thermofax screen with a selection of squeegees

The Thermofax Screen

What is a Thermofax Screen?

A thermofax is an 'old technology' machine originally designed to generate the master used to print mimeograph copies. The advent of computers made the thermofax obsolete for general office use, but artists have reclaimed the machine because of it's ability to create small silk screens with perfect detail.

The machine itself is a heat-bed that burns off the plastic coating of the mesh to the required design. The design needs to be carbon-based, which means it can be:

- a black and white laser print
- a photocopy
- an India Ink original
- pencil based (although pencils need to be tested to ensure there is sufficient carbon content).

Inkjet prints are not suitable. The image is laid against the plastic side of the mesh and this 'sandwich' is fed through the machine. Where carbon toner comes into contact with the mesh, the heat burns the mesh away to reproduce the design.

Thermofax screens are excellent for producing fine-detail or delicate textural marks such as feathers, hand writing, skeletal shapes, sketches, old documents, photographic images etc., and are an excellent alternative to photo-emulsion screens.

You don't need to own the machine to get your hands on thermofax screens. There are mail order services listed in the Resources Section – all you need to do is email or post your design to them and they'll send back a ready-to-use thermofax screen.

Advantages & Disadvantages

Thermofax screens have many advantages:

- easily accessible
- easily made
- light-weight and therefore easy on the hands (great for those suffering with arthritis or similar)
- easy to use (once good technique has been mastered)
- less messy than other tools (again, once you've developed good technique)
- easy to store (they take up much less room than traditional screens)
- the frames are re-useable when the imaged mesh has either had it's day or worn out.

The only disadvantages we can think of are:

- eventually, the mesh will break down but usually, the screen will have generated thousands of prints before this happens, and basic repairs can be achieved
- people can get addicted to them or dependent on them, and the subsequent work takes on a certain 'look' and may lose soul

Suitable Imagery
One of our books – **'Finding Your Own Visual Language'** (co-authored with Jane Dunnewold) – will provide you with many, many ways of developing your own personal imagery, but let's take a look at some examples.

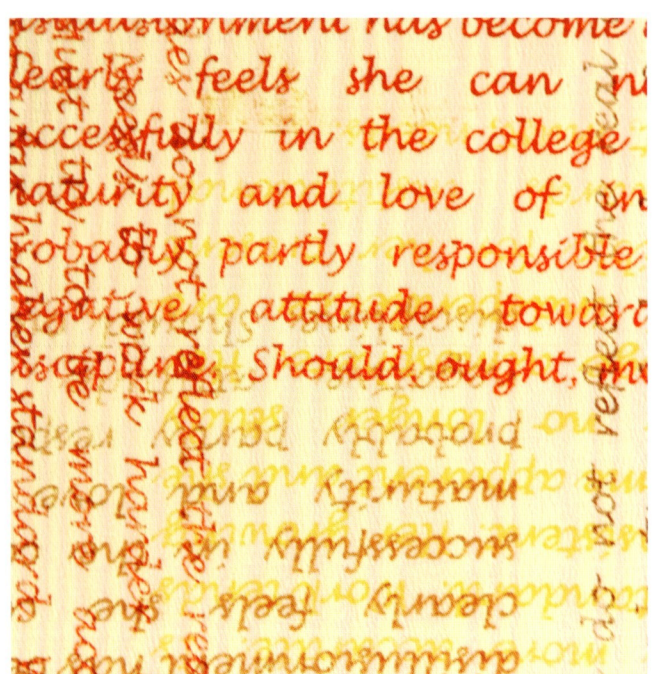

The written and/or the printed word
You can make screens based on your own handwriting, print material from the computer or copy your journal, love letters, birthday cards, postcards, recipes or old books - but do acknowledge copyright issues if your using books – make sure they're old and out of copyright protection.

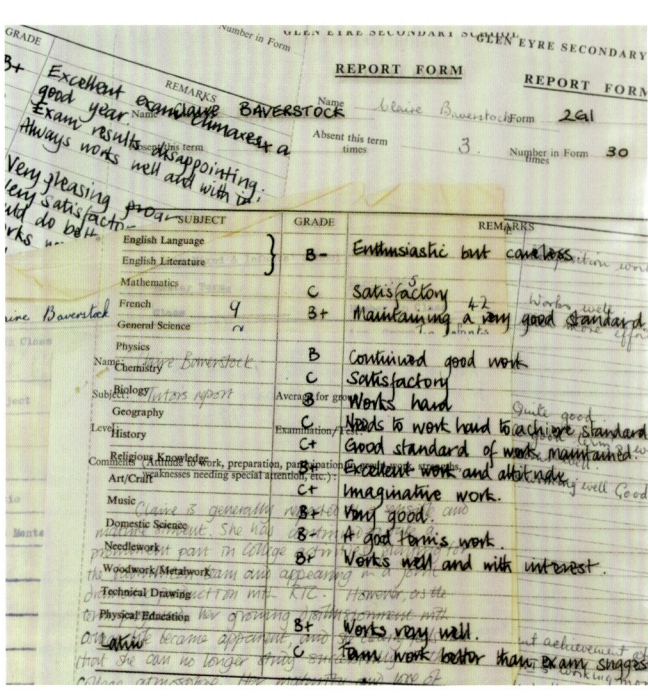

Other documentation
Maps, birth & marriage certificates, school reports, X-Rays, medical reports and so forth – all of this kind of material can make fascinating screens.

General mark-making
Any kind of mark you've made with any kind of tool on paper can be photocopied or scanned and laser printed to produce a thermofax. Imagery can be fine and delicate (such as spidery lines) or chunkier and more substantial.

Photocopies of 'stuff'
Photocopying or photographing grasses, seed heads or skeletal leaves will often yield great thermofax material, as will photocopying or photographing textural material such as thread, wool, raffia, salt, rice, lentils, seaweed etc.

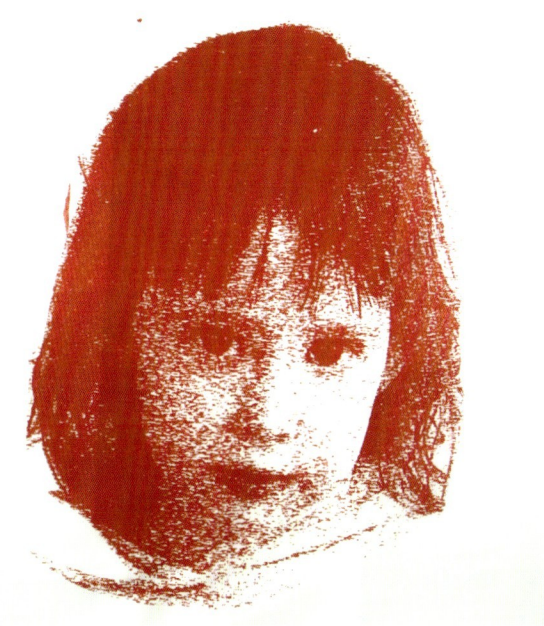

Photographic imagery
Most photographic imagery will need to be manipulated in some way as the thermofax won't handle grey scale as well as a photo-emulsion screen. Applying some kind of filter to the image or converting it by using a particular command (e.g. pen & ink) in programmes such as Photoshop will yield more interesting results.

Recognise that most photographs are rectangular in format and will print as such. It's therefore worth considering the format you're seeking to print, and making appropriate adjustments; the previous image of Lilla has had a graphic pen command applied to it, and the laserprint was then cut to leave only the outline of her head. The thorn image shown above is an example of what not to do, as it's a very chunky design and prints a rectangular format that can be hard to manage.

An alternative to using a computer programme is to make a tracing of the key elements of the photograph for use as a thermofax.

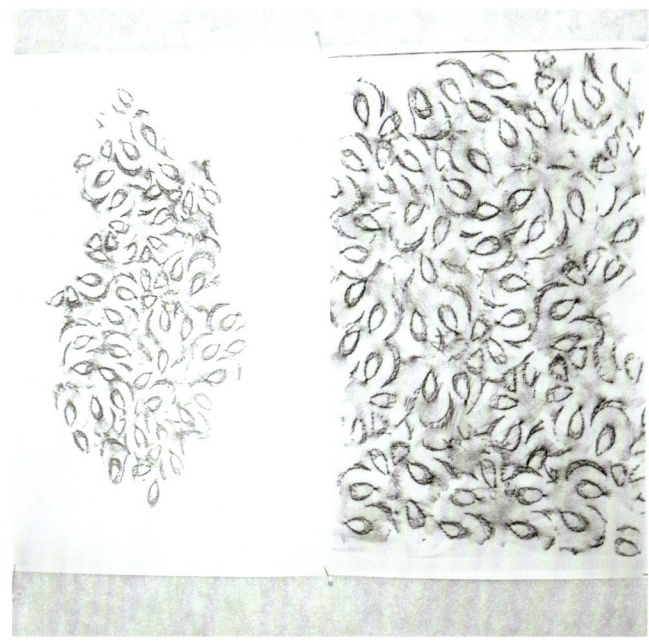

Sketches
If you're into sketching, then almost any sketch – from a life drawing to a charcoal landscape or a pen & ink drawing – can be effectively turned into a thermofax. The example shown is a drawing done by one of Claire's granddaughters.

Rubbings
Whilst you can make rubbings directly on to cloth using Markel sticks or oil pastels, this isn't always an appropriate approach. Instead, take rubbings on paper for potential use as a thermofax – it's a great way of generating a hazy, slightly disintegrating mark. The example shown is a rubbing taken from an Indian print block, which Leslie then adjusted to get rid of the square format. You'll see how it prints on page 28.

So, what to do? The solution is to take a print from your eraser stamp or print block using black acrylic or fabric paint. The photograph illustrates how different amounts of media and different pressure give different results. These prints can then be photocopied and turned into a thermofax. You can also:

- enlarge or reduce the image
- collage it with bedfellows to make a larger design (see left)
- scan it and manipulate it with a suitable programme

Iron-Offs

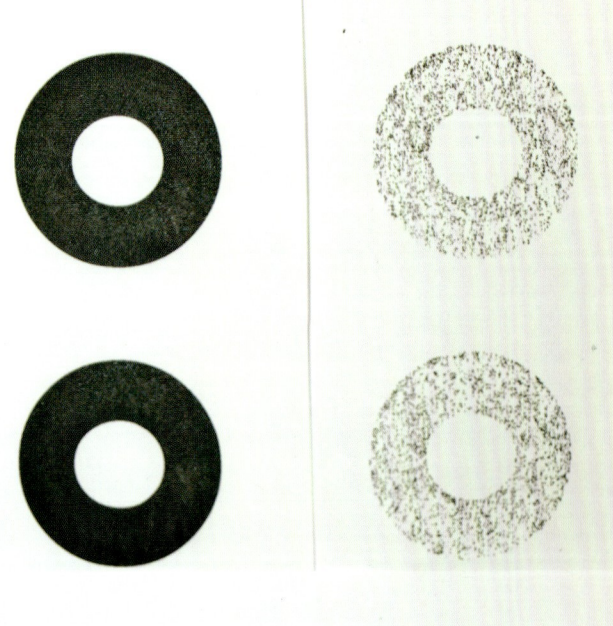

Print Blocks & Stamps

Whilst cut eraser stamps and (Indian) print blocks are a great way of getting imagery on to cloth, they can have a couple of disadvantages:

- *if eraser stamps aren't cut deep enough, they will print in a 'blobby' uneven manner*
- *although one of the joys of hand printing is that each print is different, stamping doesn't generally drive a great deal of media into the cloth, so the result can be fragile. This may be just what you want but sometimes, you're looking for the design to print in a more definite way.*
- *Indian print blocks don't always print clearly as they're often only sold once past their usable life.*

On page 14, we will discuss ironing a photocopy or laser print in order to get rid of excess toner before burning the mesh. However, we've observed that the ironed-off print can be more interesting than the original, as the example above shows. So, try this and see what you get.

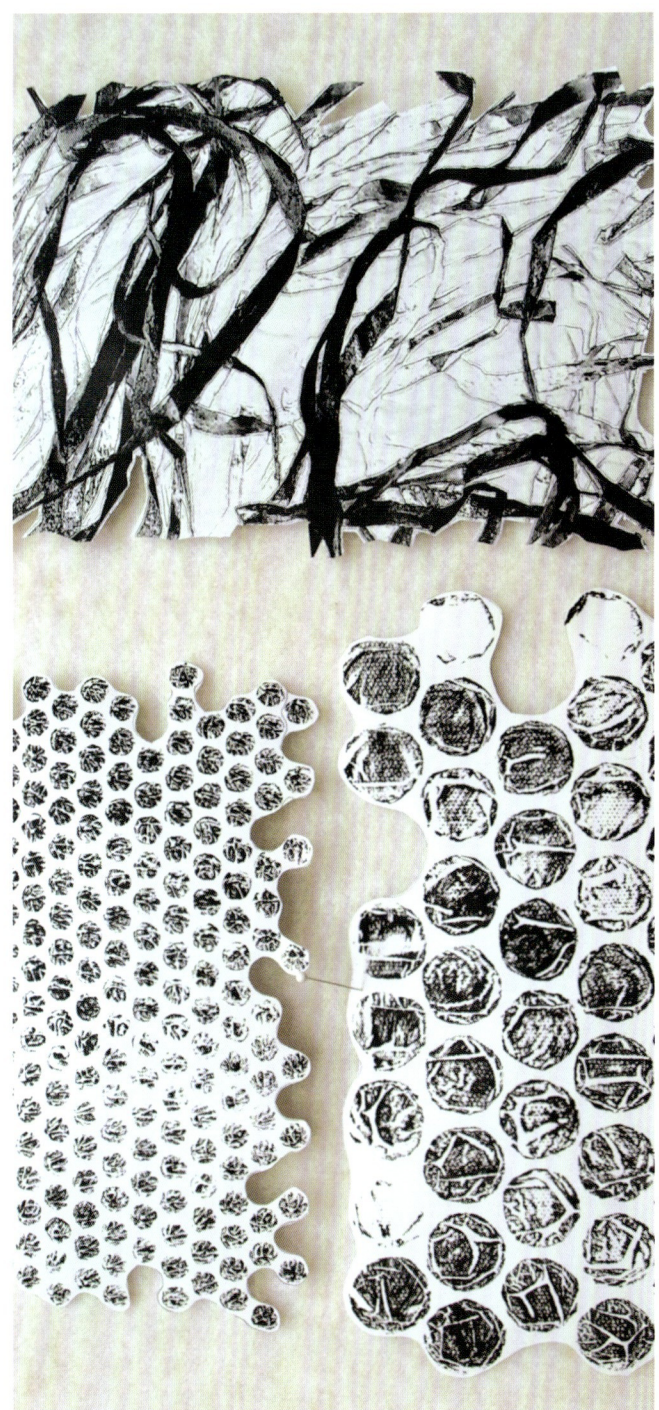

Auditioning with Acetates

Finally, try printing or copying your imagery on to acetate to audition it in the following ways:

- on background cloth; this will enable you to establish if the imagery is suitable for the composition/end result you have in mind.
- layering up imagery; you can lay acetates on top of each other (the same or different images) to see how they will look when printed on top of each other.

Adjusting Square or Rectangular Formats

As mentioned, do acknowledge that some designs (such as photographs or documents) may produce a recognisable square or rectangular print. Whilst this might be desirable and can be managed, it could be frustrating to generate rectangles if this isn't within the desired compositional feel of the cloth. Later, we'll cover how to minimise rectangular printing but for now, here are some ways of adjusting imagery to enable easier 'feathering' of edges:

- using a craft knife, slice into the four hard edges of the design you're going to use to make the burn. Focus on achieving uneven edges that will 'feather' together when printed side-by-side.
- work on the edges using a software programme such as Photoshop.
- use white acrylic paint or 'white out' correction fluid to create an uneven edge.
- reverse images; it's easy to get left and right directionality using acetates.

Ultimately, the world is your oyster and if you need more ideas, then turn to **'Finding Your Own Visual Language'**.

BURNING THE MESH, MAKING THE SCREEN

Even though you may not own a thermofax machine, it can be useful to understand how the mesh is burned to create the image. So what's needed?

The Imagery
As discussed, you'll need correctly scaled imagery in one of the following formats:

- a black and white photocopy
- a black and white laser print
- an original in India Ink
- an original in pencil or charcoal (test pencils first, as not all will work)

Do not use inkjet prints and do check the imagery is scaled to fit the size of the frame. The frame sizes vary from supplier to supplier so if you're sending off your imagery to a mail-order thermofax service, always refer to their sizing guidance. Most will accept imagery via email or by post.

The Mesh
If you are sending your imagery off to be made by a thermofax supplier, you don't need to really concern yourself with worrying about the mesh or the machine that burns the imagery. And if you own a machine already, you probably already know what's coming! But, if you're just plain curious, read on. Thermofax Mesh comes in different weights and the most suitable for textile work is 70 weight. The rolls also come in different widths and the size used will depend on the type of machine being used to make the burn. Commonly, the standard width is 11 3/4" and the rolls are 21 yards long. The mesh is cut from the roll to fit the appropriate size of frame.

The Machine
We own an old thermofax delightfully called 'The Secretary' – probably originally in use in the 1950's. It's still possible to buy second hand and reconditioned machines on ebay (which is how we obtained our first machine). Prices have increased significantly over the last few years as the word has spread and more people have been hunting them down. It's hard to estimate what a second-hand or reconditioned machine will cost these days, but expect to pay somewhere between $500-$800. And if you're outside of the U.S.A., you'll need to factor in considerable shipping costs (we got lucky, a friend brought our machine back by First Class travel!). If you don't want to trawl ebay, there are two other options:

- *PDPM/Thermocopier:* new machines are now being made by a German company. The owner is Guenther Panenka – he speaks good English so don't hesitate to get in touch to discuss pricing and delivery. Guenther also stocks frames and mesh and may be able to supply you with spare parts for older machines. Web addresses are: www.pdpm.de or www.thermocopier.com.
- *Welsh Products:* based in the U.S.A., Welsh often have a selection of reconditioned machines and also sell mesh and frames. The web address is www.welshproducts.com.

A roll of thermofax mesh with a selection of different frames

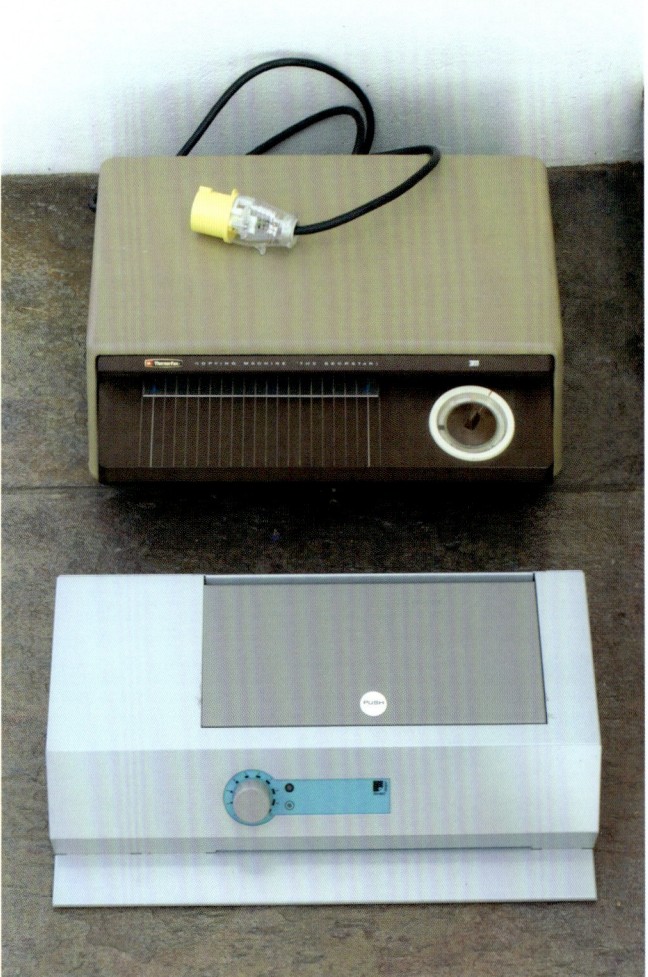

'The Secretary' - our 1950's thermofax machine is shown at the back with the new PDPM model at the front

The mesh is placed shiny-side down against the carbon image before being fed into the machine

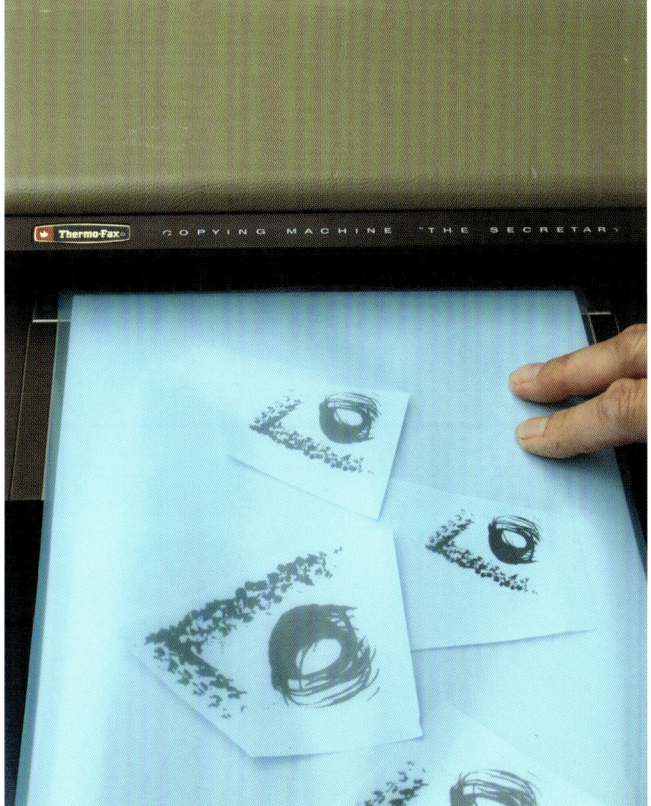

If different images or versions of imagery are being used to make a single thermofax, glue them to a piece of paper and then make the burn

So, let's assume you have the imagery, the mesh, the machine and the frames (if using frames). Time to burn! Before burning, here are a couple of points to consider:

- Most machines (including the old ones) have a dial on the front that speeds up or slows down the speed at which the mesh and its accompanying image is fed through the heat bed. At a faster speed, the burn receives less heat. Slower speeds mean more heat. Generally speaking, fine lines require a slower speed to enable more heat and dark, solid areas require a faster speed so they get less heat. You will need to experiment a little with your own machine to find out what speed works best with different kinds of images.
- High contrast is better than a lot of grey scale
- All printers and copiers are slightly different, and some will produce prints/copies that work more effectively than others.
- Lots of solid dark areas may not burn well, particularly if the copy/print is fresh. There are several ways to manage this:
    - use 5-day old copies/prints to allow the toner time to settle.
    - iron the copy/print onto several sheets of paper to get rid of excess or loose toner (and take a good look at the ironed-off image as you might prefer it to the original!)
    - experiment with the toner settings on your printer or photocopier to see what gets the best results.
    - increase the speed of the machine – this means the toner on the image is being exposed to less heat.
- Fine delicate lines are generally burned at a slower speed.

The accompanying DVD to this book will give you a clear demonstration of burning the mesh, but in brief the procedure is as follows:

- cut the mesh according to the size of frame you're using
- place the carbon-based imagery face up on a table
- place the mesh - shiny (plastic) side down - on top of the image, positioning it centrally
- set the speed dial to the appropriate setting for the imagery
- gently feed the mesh/paper sandwich into the machine; most machines 'grab' the sandwich and the rollers then feed it through; out to the back (new machines) or around and back down to the front (older machines).
- allow things to cool down a little and then peel the paper away from the mesh to reveal the burned out image.

We generally don't use a carrier for burning the mesh but if you're seeking to burn a collage of different images, here's what we do:

- arrange the imagery on a piece of photocopy paper, making sure it's going to fit into the frame area of the mesh.
- once you're satisfied with your arrangement, use a dab of glue to secure each element of the collage on to the paper.
- position the cut mesh (shiny side down) over the collage and feed it through the machine.

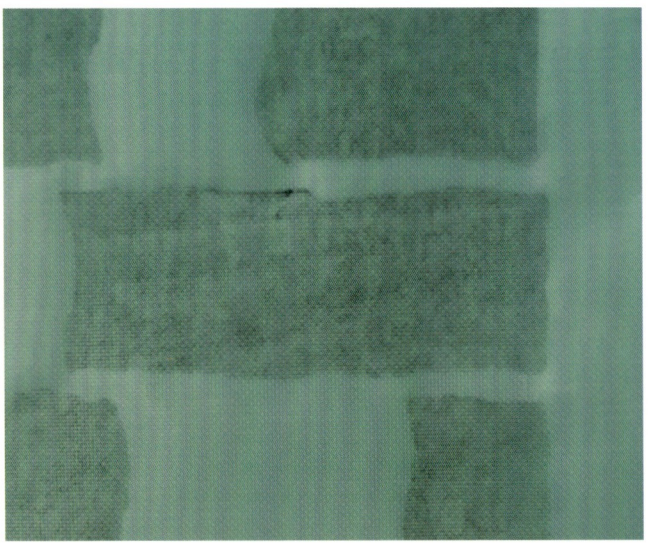

A poor burn as a result of using a very fresh photocopy

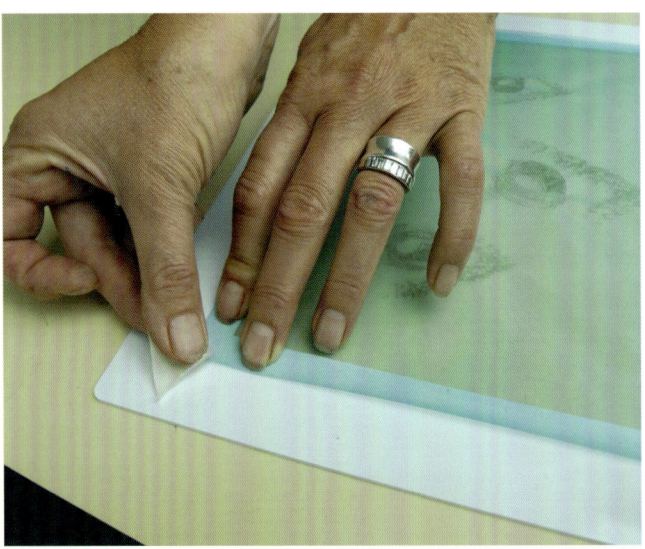

Securing the 4 corners of the mesh to the frame

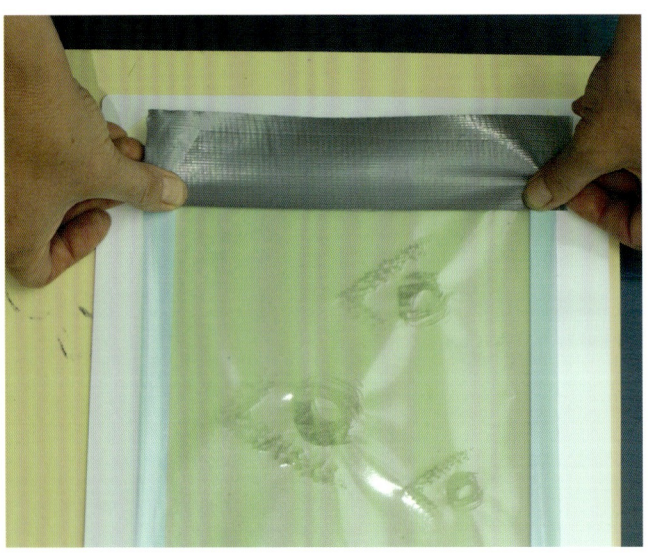

Using duct tape to secure the short sides first

Troubleshooting

And what if you don't get good burn results? This is a hard question to answer without knowing more about the machine, the image and the speed of burn. But, the following points may help:

- The image hasn't burned at all; you're not using carbon-based imagery. Remember, inkjet prints won't work.
- The image has burned a little, but not enough; the speed dial may have been set too fast for the image. If you've only peeled off a corner of the paper to take a peek, re-burn.
- The image has over-burned, toner residue (black) seems to have coloured the exposed mesh, the print/copy is hard to peel off and/or the mesh has become very crinkly; these problems tend to mainly occur when burning prints with lots of solid black on them. Remember to try the pointers provided earlier:

    - use 5-day old copies/prints to allow the toner time to settle.
    - iron the copy/print onto several sheets of paper to get rid of excess or loose toner.
    - experiment with the toner settings on your printer or photocopier to see what gets the best results, or try the 'toner save' setting
    - increase the speed of the machine – this means the toner is being exposed to less heat.

Generally speaking, we tend not to use thermofax screens to generate chunky, shape-based imagery. It's often just as effective to make a temporary stencil for a traditional silkscreen and our book **'Screen Printing; layering textiles with colour, texture & imagery'** provides you with 23 approaches to making temporary screen stencils. But, you'll need to experiment to see what works for you, and what doesn't.

Taping up the Mesh

We prefer to tape our imaged mesh into ready-made plastic frames as we find this generates the best results. Some people like to attach the mesh to the frame using double-sided tape, but we prefer waterproof tape such as Duck. Here's how we do it (and take a look at the images as well):

- Position the mesh centrally on the frame, shiny side up.
- Use a small piece of masking tape to anchor each corner.
- Starting with the short sides, cut lengths of Duck tape and position them so they grab a decent amount of mesh but don't encroach on to the burned imagery. Repeat with the long sides.

- Flip the frame over and use more Duck tape, positioning it to line up with the tape on the other side.
- Thermofaxes are generally used shiny (plastic) side down as the action of drawing the squeegee across the plastic may speed up it's deterioration. We usually mark the rough side of the mesh on the screen frame; if you can see the mark (we generally write 'this side up'), the thermofax is the right way up.

To save money, some people prefer not to use thermofax frames. Instead, they use duct tape to reinforce the edges of the mesh. However, we observe that printing with a 'floppy' thermofax tends to generate mess – unless you've developed superb technique! A viable option is to attach the mesh to a traditional silkscreen. If you opt to do this, don't reinforce the edges of the thermofax mesh with Duck tape as it's thick and creates a gap between the thermofax and the screen mesh – making printing harder.

Instead, reinforce the edges of the thermofax mesh with masking tape (which can be soaked off on washing), or use acrylic paint to reinforce a 1" band around the edges. Then, tape the thermofax mesh to the back of a silkscreen using masking tape (take a look at the picture). Whilst this approach is a little more time-consuming, we believe it generates a better quality print than a floppy thermofax.

Using the Thermofax Screen

OVERVIEW OF MEDIA

We've gone into more detail (and included recipes and projects) on pages 37 to 50, but we thought it would help to provide an overview of the media you could use.

Procion-Type, Fibre-Reactive Thickened Mx Dye Paints

Fibre-reactive Mx dyes are suitable for all natural-fibre fabrics except wool. They are mixed with several ingredients to transform them into paints and need a chemical additive in the form of Sodium Carbonate (commonly referred to as Soda Ash) in order to bond with the fibre and fix permanently. A huge range of colours is available, and guidance and recipes are given on pages 47 to 50.

Discharge Paste

Discharging agents are used to remove colour from cloth. Most of the off-the-shelf products (such as Jacquard Discharge Paste) are formulated to remove colour from Mx dyed fabric. Whilst we have used Jacquard, we now prefer to make our own discharge paste using a chemical called Formosol. It's mixed in a little warm water and then added to the same print paste used for making thickened dyes. More detailed information and recipes are given on pages 42 and 43.

Black commercial fabrics will often discharge – some are manufactured specifically as dischargeable fabrics. However, not every piece of black cloth you buy will discharge, so it's important to test it first before buying an entire roll!

Thermofax screens can be used with a wide range of media

Fabric Paints & Acrylics

Fabric paints sit with the acrylic family, but are manufactured specifically for use with fabric, rather than paper. Drying retardants and surfactants (wetting agents) are usually added to them and a good fabric paint should not alter the hand of the cloth in the same manner as an acrylic paint.

One key advantage of fabric paints is that they sit on the surface of the cloth and don't require chemicals to fix them. Instead, they're bonded to the surface of the cloth by heat-setting with a dry iron. Another advantage is that they are generally very light-fast. A huge range of ready-mixed colours are available in both transparent and opaque hues, and you can also opt to buy pigment and mix it into a polymer fabric binder or transparent base extender.

Fabric paints are easy to use but they **must not be left to dry out in a thermofax, silkscreen, or on any of your tools**. If they do, they will seal the screen mesh or stiffen/glue together bristles permanently, so wash up the second you finish working with them. More detailed information and guidance on use is given on pages 44 and 45, but always read the manufacturers' instructions carefully.

Multiple layers of printing using the same thermofax

Developing Good Technique

It's very important to develop competent technique. Whilst there may be occasions where poor technique yields interesting results, perfecting technique is important as it builds confidence and allows you to refine the images you're printing. Good technique will also enable crisp, clearly defined prints.

- Pin out your cloth: as you pull the wet media across the thermofax it passes through the imaged mesh and on to the cloth, which creates the print. When you pick the thermofax up, the cloth can stick to the mesh, so pinning down the cloth before you print is important. Lay out the cloth and send ball-headed pins straight through to the drop cloth and into the felt underneath. Push the pin right up to it's ball-head or T as then you'll be able to place a thermofax on top safely. Put the cloth under some tension as you pin it out as it will stretch somewhat as it gets wet with media.
- Whilst theromfax printing is normally undertaken on dry cloth, working wet-on-wet cloth can yield very interesting results:

    - to work on damp cloth, spin out the excess soda solution in a spin dryer or washing machine, then pin it to your print board on a drop cloth.
    - to work really wet, place sheet plastic on to your print board, squeeze out the excess soda solution then place the wet cloth on to the plastic; use clamps to hold it in place or pin if you don't mind a few tiny holes in the plastic.

- Wear well-fitting gloves. A common problem with thermofax printing is unwanted finger smudges, caused when picking up the thermofax and re-positioning it. To avoid this, either wear surgical gloves, or make sure you're wearing gloves that fit properly – avoid using gloves that have dangly bits at the end of your fingers! If you're printing with fabric paint or acrylics, don't wear gloves.
- Having organised the fabric, position the thermofax shiny side (back side) down for your first print; neither in the middle of the cloth, nor on the edge (you'll work off the edges later). The thermofax is generally used shiny side down as the action of drawing the squeegee across the plastic may speed up it's deterioration. We usually mark the rough side of the mesh on the screen frame; if you can see the mark, the thermofax is the right way up.

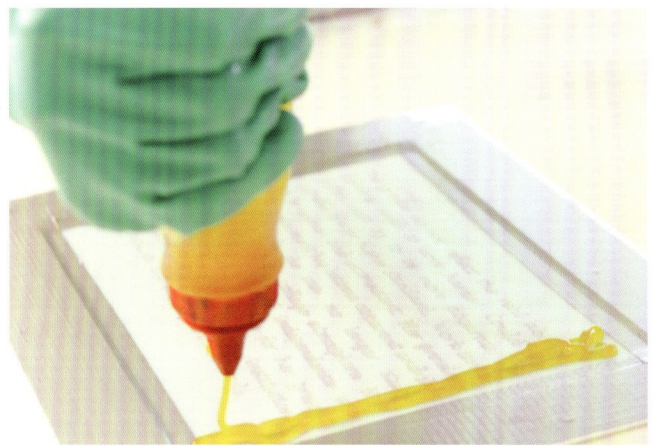

- Spoon/pour the chosen media at the top or right-hand side (if you're right-handed) of the thermofax – this is called a **bead**.

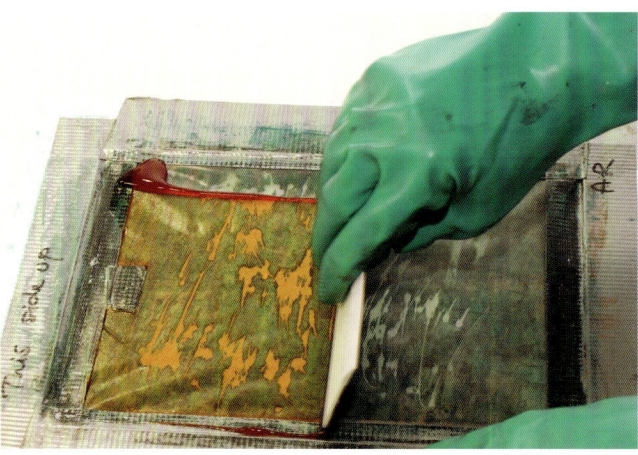

- Pulling the squeegee towards you, or from right to left (if right-handed) is the best way to achieve a smooth, even print… and practise helps too.
- Keep the squeegee just off the vertical as you pull. Try not to lean it towards you too much as close to upright generates a crisp print.

- When you get to the other end of the thermofax, don't push the squeegee back in the opposite direction. Instead, ease up the pressure and scoop the unused media onto the squeegee so you can deposit it in the best place for your next pull.

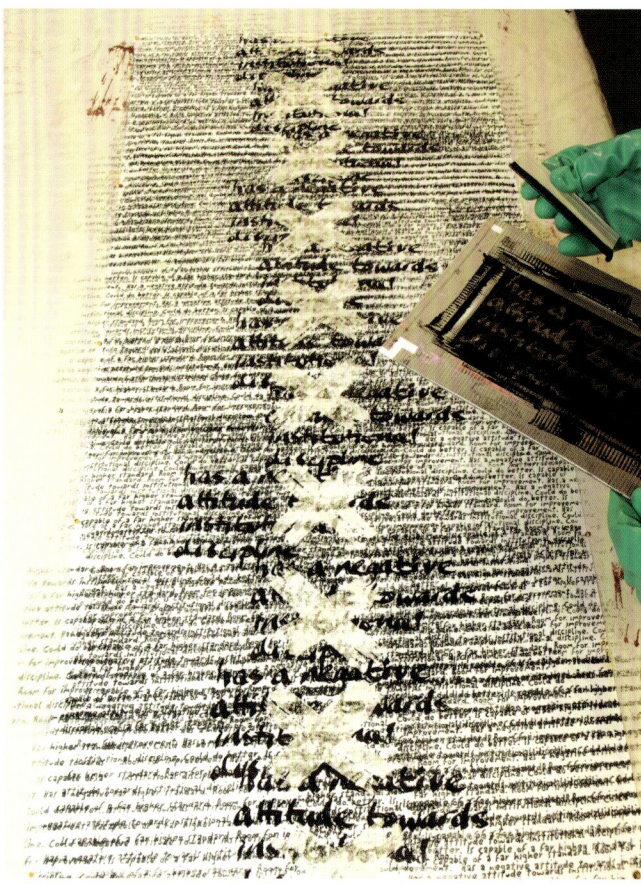

- **Tip:** keep the squeegee over the thermofax as you re-position it, otherwise you might get unwanted drips on your cloth.
- How many **pulls** you need will depend on your own physical strength and the fabric you're using; a fine silk may only need one pull, with fairly light pressure. Heavy cotton may need more pulls with harder pressure. It takes practice to get your print as you want it. As you print, add more media as necessary – the quantity of media is again determined by the cloth and the effect you want. Generally speaking, we'd estimate that one or two pulls will be sufficient in most cases.
- Pay attention to the amount of media left on the thermofax after each pull, and top up as necessary. Position the thermofax on the cloth BEFORE you add more media.

- If you need to pause during printing, place the thermofax and the squeegee on a cat litter tray – don't leave it sitting on your cloth.

The quality of print you get is determined by several variables, either singly or in combination:

- *the fabric type;* fine weights (sheers and light pongees), medium weights (cotton, silk-cotton), heavy weights (felt, heavy cottons/linen). The finer the fabric, the fewer passes required to make a clean print.
- *the wet media;* the consistency of the media has an impact; very thick media requires more pressure. Too watery a consistency results in bleeding and blurring.
- *the pressure you exert;* how hard you press down as you pull the squeegee is directly related to the amount of media deposited on the surface of the cloth.
- *the number of pulls;* generally speaking, one or two pulls will be sufficient, but since all of the factors are related, it's a good idea to test fabric and wet media before you work on your good-quality cloth.

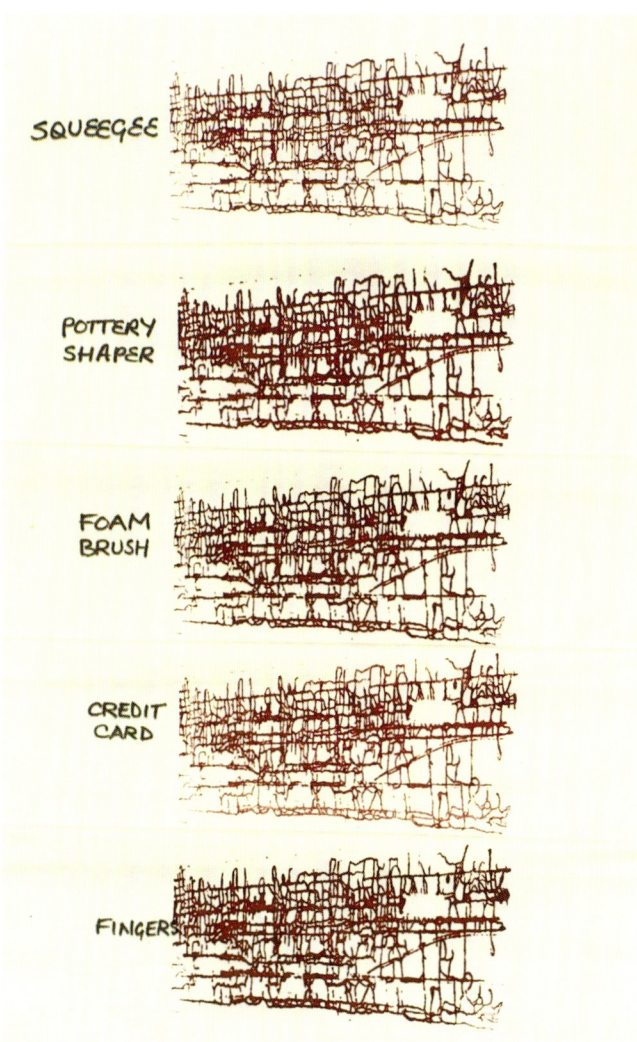

We've also tested alternatives to using a squeegee to make a print as we're aware that people can struggle to develop good technique with a squeegee. The photograph shows the results we've achieved with five different tools. At first glance they appear very similar, but if you look closely, the prints made using a squeegee and a credit card are the crispest and finest.

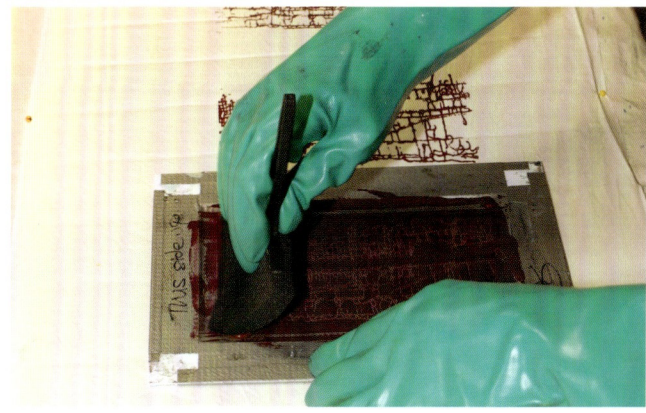

Ultimately, you need to practise on different fabric types and with different media in order to understand the variables and gain some level of proficiency in using them. When you're printing a whole piece of cloth (as opposed to laying down a single, accent print), try to remember to print right off the edge of the cloth to avoid a 'frame' around the edge.

Practise your technique on a drop cloth to see the results of different pressure and different numbers of pulls. It can be a good idea to always make your first print on to the dropcloth or a piece of waste cloth to make sure the thermofax is 'open' and printing well before you get to your good cloth.

Our advice would be:
- if the thermofax is of a fine, delicate line design, use a squeegee, spreader or credit card.
- if the imagery is chunky or shape-based, then test using a pottery scraper, foam brush or even your fingers.

'Ghosting'

Ghosting happens when the thermofax is placed onto a wet print; the media is picked up on the back of the thermofax and will transfer itself back down onto the fabric when you place the screen for the next print. The mark will be fragile and often incomplete - hence the term 'ghosting'.

We find that ghosting isn't generally an issue with a thermofax as the fine-line imagery tends to lay down 'dry' prints. However, we acknowledge that we're likely to be more practised than a novice and when working on small pieces of fabric with chunkier imagery, ghosting can still happen. Ghosting can either provide added texture, or create a mess – it depends on what you're trying to achieve. On larger pieces of cloth, ghosting can usually be avoided by keeping the prints apart to begin with, then going back and printing in the spaces between. If you're printing a close-up, repeat pattern, you can also lay a piece of paper towel down over the previous wet print to prevent ghosting, but be careful not to leave it on the wet media (particularly fabric paint) in case it gets permanently stuck there.

Ghosting can also be avoided by taking breaks in the printing process; make as many separate prints as you can and then stop. Wash and dry the thermofax, let the media dry off and then return to continue printing. In the interim, occupy yourself with something else, such as working on another piece of cloth, documenting your process or undertaking visual imagery work. Weather can effect how fast media dries and warm weather generally makes life much easier in the textile world!

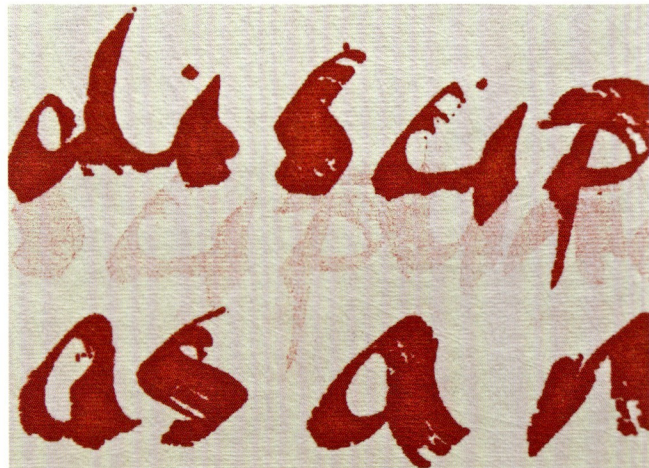

An example of 'ghosting'

Managing Squares/Rectangles

If you've produced a thermofax with a square or rectangular edge, you have two options:

- use the square or rectangular format deliberately (as shown in the photograph on the left)
- over-print; if you print a square or rectangular format over and over on itself, eventually it won't read.

Clean-Up

Wash the thermofax with cold or luke-warm water (not hot) and a soft sponge – do not use an abrasive such as a scouring pad or a brush as you'll damage the plastic coating on the mesh. Some paints can stain the mesh, but if the water's running clear, your thermofax is probably clean. Dry it by laying it between two layers of old towel. Gently pat the mesh and try not to rub it, as this may damage the plastic coating. Wipe down the frame edge thoroughly, and squeeze the edges of the duck tape to make sure any media that may have found it's way underneath is squeezed out.

Never leave **any** media drying on the thermofax. If you want to use the thermofax repeatedly but need time for the media to dry in between layers of print, wash and dry it. Never allow it to sit with media on it. The mesh dries quickly, so the screen will be ready to use again in a few minutes. If necessary, use a fan to speed drying time.

Store thermofax screens upright and away from heat or direct sunlight. Use them considerately and they'll reward you with hundreds of prints.

Wash the thermofax carefully in running cold water and a soft sponge or cloth - DO NOT use a brush or scrubber!

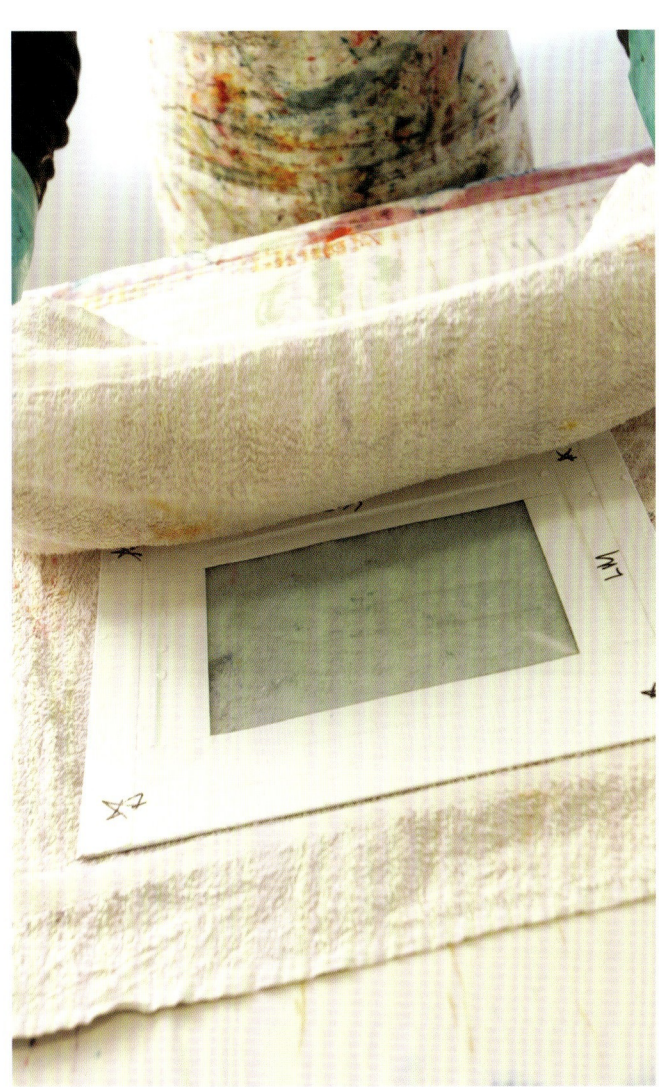

Pat the thermofax dry with a towel

Use a towel to squeeze out any water that may have got underneath the duct tape

Has a negative attitude towards institutional discipline. Could do better. Is capable of a far higher standard. Room for improvement.

DESIGN ADJUSTMENTS & REPAIRS

The design on any thermofax can be adjusted temporarily or permanently and repairs can be made to deteriorating plastic. Let's take a look at this.

Temporary Adjustments

The key thing to remember when making a temporary design adjustment is to avoid using anything that could tear or damage the plastic coating of the mesh. If this happens, your design will have been permanently altered. In our experience, the most effective temporary adjustment uses a double layer of kitchen towel, secured with masking tape to the edge of the frame:

- Tear off a piece of kitchen paper and fold it in half, or to a size suitable for the area to be masked.
- You may need to cut into the paper layers to fine-tune the mask.
- Position the double layer of kitchen paper on the shiny side (back) of the thermofax. Temporary masks are always fixed to the back of the screen as otherwise, the action of the squeegee could drive media under the mask.
- Use masking tape to fix the paper towel mask to the frame edges – *do not* use masking tape directly on the plastic mesh as it can tear on removal.
- Print in the usual manner and take off the mask when you wash the screen.

Permanent Adjustments and/or Repairs

Sometimes you can make a thermofax that isn't quite right, but with some adjustment, could be right. You could of course burn a new thermofax, but this seems wasteful and costly. Instead, try making repairs using heavy-body acrylic paint.

- Consider the adjustments you want to make.
- Suspend the thermofax on a cat litter tray.
- Using a fine brush, carefully paint out the areas you need to. Do this slowly; avoid trying to fill the exposed mesh in one go. If you try to do this, we find that thick blobs of paint tend to spread and bleed into unwanted areas. Instead, have the patience to apply several (up to 5) thin layers of paint, letting each layer dry out completely between coats.
- On completion, your thermofax wil have been permanently altered.
- This is a great way to 'fix' a design that's printing a strong rectangle or square shape; simply feather in the edges using paint.

Painting in with acrylic paint is also the approach we use to mend a thermofax that's starting to disintegrate. You'll realise a thermofax is breaking down by either noticing that it's printing differently, or noticing that the plastic is starting to lift and tear away in places. All thermofaxes will eventually disintegrate, but usually only after thousands of prints. Sometimes ours break down in a very pleasing manner in which case, we just carry on using the 'new' design. However, if you wish to try and halt any disintegration or repair a screen, use acrylic paint to fill any torn/exposed areas.

Here we're taping cut paper towel to create a temporary mask on the back (shiny side) of the screen

We can now print a portion of the screen safely

Making a permanent repair using acrylic paint

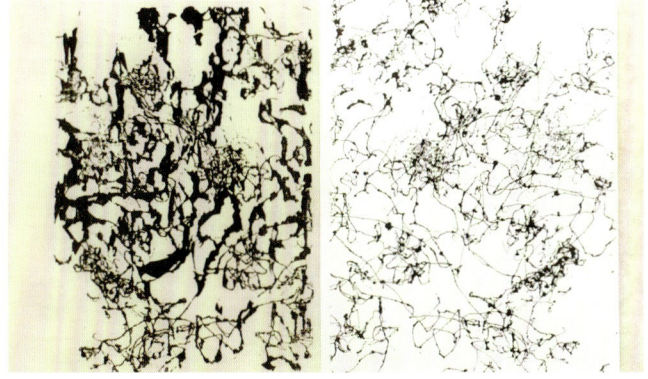

Some screens breakdown in a useful manner - the image on the right shows the original. On the left, you'll see how the image is breaking down, but in a very useable manner

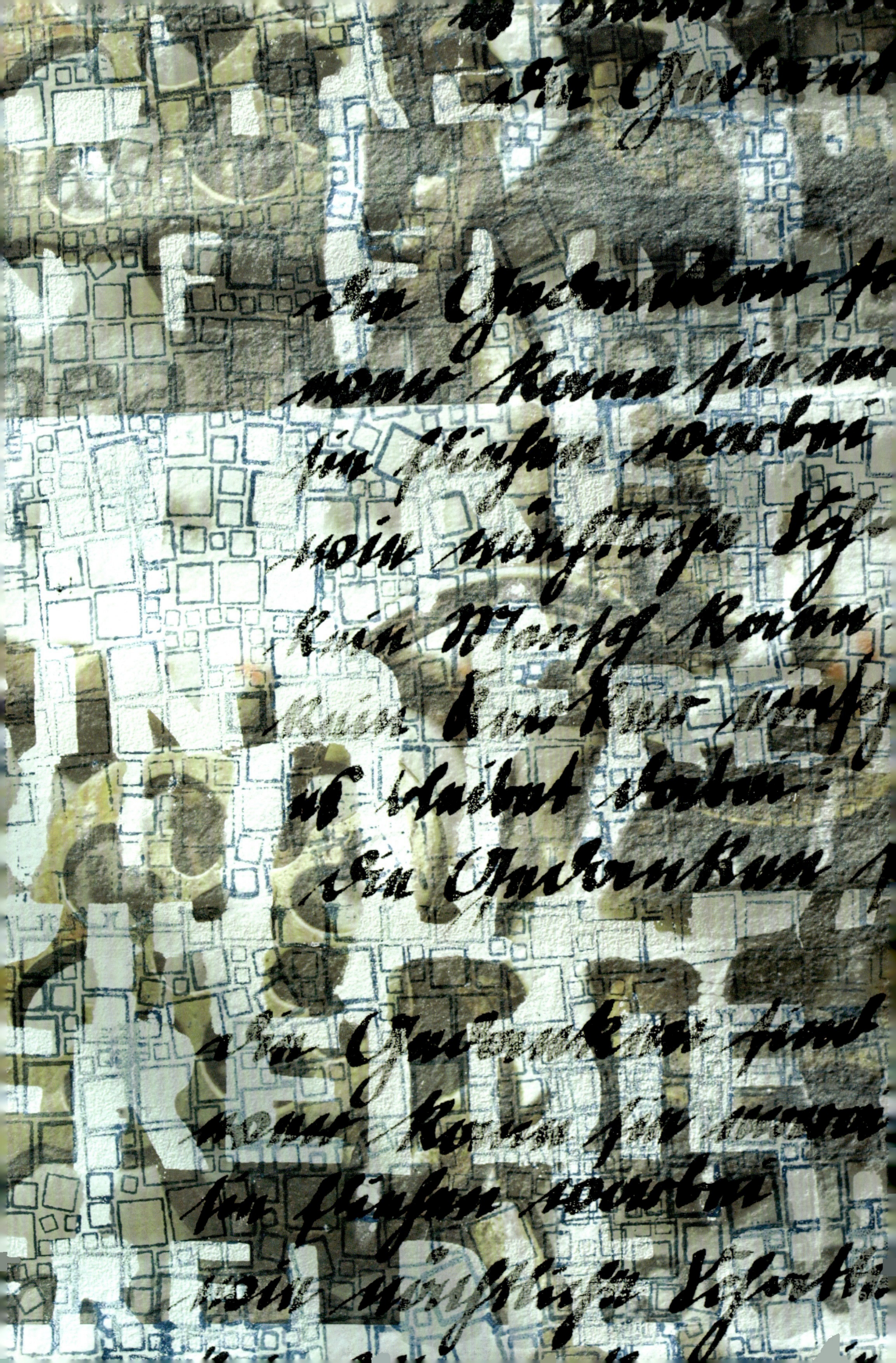

Projects - Exploring Ways Forward

We wanted to include some 'projects' to help you build experience and encourage you to explore. Just like any other skill, printing with a thermofax can take time to master and you'll need to practise and suspend judgement on your early results.

One key thing to remember is that it's rare for a piece of cloth to look brilliant after a single process, particularly compositional wholecloth. Compositional cloth will often need between three and eight layers of process to become complete, so bear this in mind and don't get too judgemental after process one! Cloth that's destined to be cut up and re-structured (as in quilt-making) can hit the mark after one process, but will often be more successful after several.

However, it's important to stress that layering multiple wet processes doesn't happen all at once. If you're working with thickened dye paints, the soda present in the cloth will only be capable of handling a finite quantity of dye. As such, the cloth will need to be batched, rinsed, dried and re-soaked in soda for the next process. It can take many days – and sometimes weeks – to build layer upon layer. And in between processes, it's important to iron your work-in-progress, pin it up and really look at it.

A NOTE ON COMPOSITION

When trying to decide on your next move, consider the following:

- *Figure-Ground;* the term 'figure-ground refers to the sense of foreground (figure) and background (ground). Achieving a sense of figure-ground is vitally important as it will generate depth and provide…
- *Visual interest;* visual interest is often driven through the use of contrasting elements. Contrast can be achieved through colour, value, texture, shape, line, scale, mass, void and so forth.
- *A sense of cohesion;* whilst contrast is important and can range from the subtle to the almost garish, it's important that design and compositional elements have a sense of belonging and have relationship with each other. Just as with contrast, relationships can be driven through the use of value, colour, scale, texture, line and shape. So for example, you may be driving contrast using a change of scale by adding a larger design element to the piece, but that element could be a larger version of a shape already present in the cloth… which will build relationship at the same time.
- *Background & Perspective;* generally speaking, we observe that students find it easier to start building background (the 'ground' in figure-ground) before tackling the foreground (the figure) or very strong compositional elements. Take a look at the cloth and ask yourself; "am I done with the background yet, does the background have enough depth and interest?". If so, start planning the foreground (figure) element(s) of the piece.
- *Colour;* Colour use is important when building contrast and relationship. For example, you can work in a close colour range, in a monochromatic theme or in high contrast compositions using complementary colours.
- *Value;* varying a single colour from light to dark can create shadows, movement and depth.
- *Transparency;* use pale value dye paint mixtures or transparent fabric paints to achieve subtle elements and to allow what's beneath to gleam through. Discharge can also achieve this for you.
- *Opacity;* use opaque fabric paints to generate contrast, beef up impact and to emphasise a sense of an image being 'on top' or obviously foreground.
- *Imagery;* what addition will move the piece forward? Think line, texture and shape. Relationship is key.
- *Scale;* what size imagery works best? Do you need to include a range of different sizes of mark? This is particularly important if you're trying to develop a sense of perspective.

And remember, you can always audition a new image by printing or drawing on to acetate and laying it on top of the cloth.

So, lots for you to think about and **'Finding Your Own Visual Language'** will provide you with more detail if this is an area you're interested in developing. In the meantime, try having a go at some or all of the following 'projects' to get you started.

The Projects

For simplicity, we've based most of the exercises on thickened dye paints. You can of course use fabric paints but acknowledge that with multiple layers, they will have an impact on the hand of the fabric. Refer to the recipes on pages 37 to 41 to make the paints or discharge paste. And remember, for any of these exercises, you don't have to use primaries. Try creating more complex colours using the recipes provided on pages 47 to 50.

Before you start, prepare your cloth by scouring it and soda soaking it. We'd recommend you try these exercises on dry cloth and move on to experiment with printing on damp or wet cloth if you want to explore the impact of bleed. From time to time, vary the size and shape of your cloth; the format could be square, rectangular or very long and thin, but work on something of a reasonable size.

We suggest you follow the exercises fairly closely to begin with as we've observed that the learning tends to be easier. Having done them once, you can take things further by mixing different elements of different exercises together. When you get to this stage, the key question to keep asking is "what if..?". Try making a note of what you think will happen, then undertake your experiment and see if you were right. But don't worry if you weren't – that's what experimentation is all about – learning and discovering.

Once background has been achieved, the options you'll have to develop the compositional elements of your cloth will be myriad. It's important to take time to look, think and audition ideas but as a prompt, we've included a few suggestions with some of the exercises.

There are 9 projects in total, and the first four start with un-dyed cloth as we believe this will help you to understand the outcome more clearly. You could then repeat the projects on a piece of hand-dyed cloth in a pale value.

Print with contrasting imagery in the strongest value of the background colour, or a different colour

1. LAYERING VALUE

This exercise involves printing the cloth three times with the same thermofax in three different values of a single colour, moving from pale, to medium to dark. Pick the imagery you want to use; it could be textural, line or shape-based, organic or geometric etc.

- Choose a colour you wish to use for the background, and make 250ml as a thickened dye paint. This will be your strongest value dye – 'Pot 3'.
- Spoon a quarter of 'Pot 3' into another pot (Pot 2) – how much you'll need will depend on the size of the piece you're working on, and the design you're printing with. For example, a very 'open' design with lots of space will need more dye paint than a more delicate design. Don't sweat the amounts too much and don't get twitchy about having to match the dye if you run out – approximates are okay!
- Add twice as much print paste to the dye paint in 'Pot 2' and stir well – you've now reduced the strength down to 25% of Pot 3: a 1 to 4 ratio of dye paint to print paste. Give this pot a '2' label.
- Now take a quarter of the paint in 'Pot 2' and put it in yet another pot. Add twice as much print paste and stir well – you've now reduced the strength down to 10-12% of Pot 3: a 1 to 8 ratio of dye paint to print paste. Label this pot '1'.
- Start printing with Pot 1; the weakest value. Aim to print all over the cloth but don't worry too much about getting a perfectly even distribution – some variation can add interest. Remember to work off the edges. Don't worry about ghosting.
- Now print all over the cloth again, using Pot 2.
- Finish by printing a final layer using Pot 3.
- Batch your cloth for a minimum of 4 hours (ideally overnight), then rinse, dry and contemplate it. You should have made a good start to a background and can now think about how to move the piece forward.

Note; you can achieve greater jumps in value change if you increase the ratios of print paste to dye – just remember, the more print paste you add to the pre-mixed dye, the paler the value. Some hues will also change to a different colour as they get paler. For example, we find that the Black we use strikes to a blue-green when diluted with print paste. Magenta tends to drop down to pink and Rust Orange will often strike to a pale peach/apricot.

So, you'll have created a background consisting of 3 values of a single colour – which should already be generating depth on the cloth. Here are some prompts to help you decide on ways forward:

- significantly increase the scale of the imagery used to create the background. Consider colour and placement (think about the impact and balance you want to achieve) and using pieces of cloth, paper or acetates audition several placements of this new, chunkier image. When you're happy, get going and do it for real on the cloth.
- develop new but related imagery to create the figure or foreground elements. Print it in a darker version of the colour used for the background, or consider using a complementary or analgous colour.

2. LAYERING COLOUR(S)

This exercise has many variations and involves printing a background with two or three colours. Your colour choices are enormous, but some examples might include:

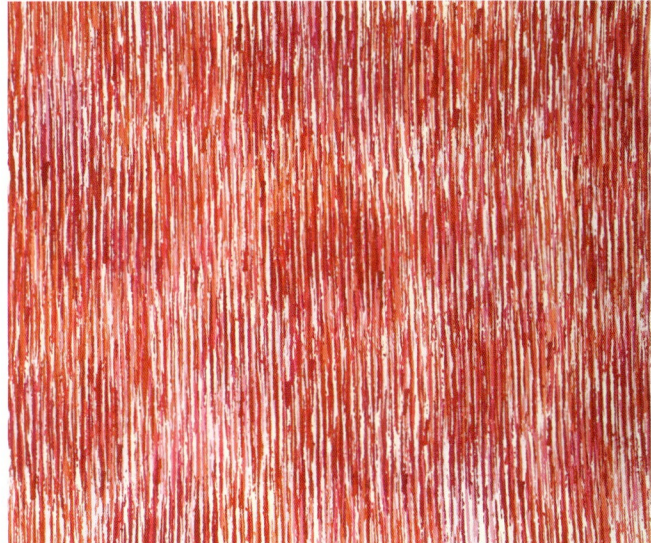

- A single hue: for example, you may want a background of blue, but that background can contain many different blues. You could print in Turquoise, followed by Royal Blue. You could print in Turquoise or Royal, and then use Black – the black we use has a bluey-green bias, so we can cheat! You could print in all three; Turquoise, Royal and Black. The example above shows cloth printed with different reds.

- Analogous colour scheme: an analogous colour scheme has colours in it that are close to each other. For example, yellow and orange, orange and red, red and purple, purple and blue, blue and green and as the example on the right shows, yellow and green.

- Complementary colour scheme: pick colours that are opposite to each other. For example: blue and orange, yellow and purple, red and green (as above).
- Triadic colour scheme: here, you print with all three primaries (Red, Yellow and Blue), or all three Secondaries (Orange, Purple and Green).

Chose your colour scheme and mix the thickened dyes in your chosen range of colours. To print:

- Consider your colours and start with the one that's likely to be most easily bullied by the other colours. For example, yellow tends to be more quickly adulterated than red (particularly if the red is magenta). So start with the yellow and move on to print the other colour(s).
- Alternatively, start with the colour that you wish to have the most dominance in the piece as you'll then be able to print other colours on top with due consideration.
- Print three to six layers, then batch the cloth. Rinse, iron and pin up to contemplate your next move.

The next 3 images provide an example of printing a Triadic (3 primaries) colour scheme;

- Leslie started with yellow
- then printed with blue, which generated greens

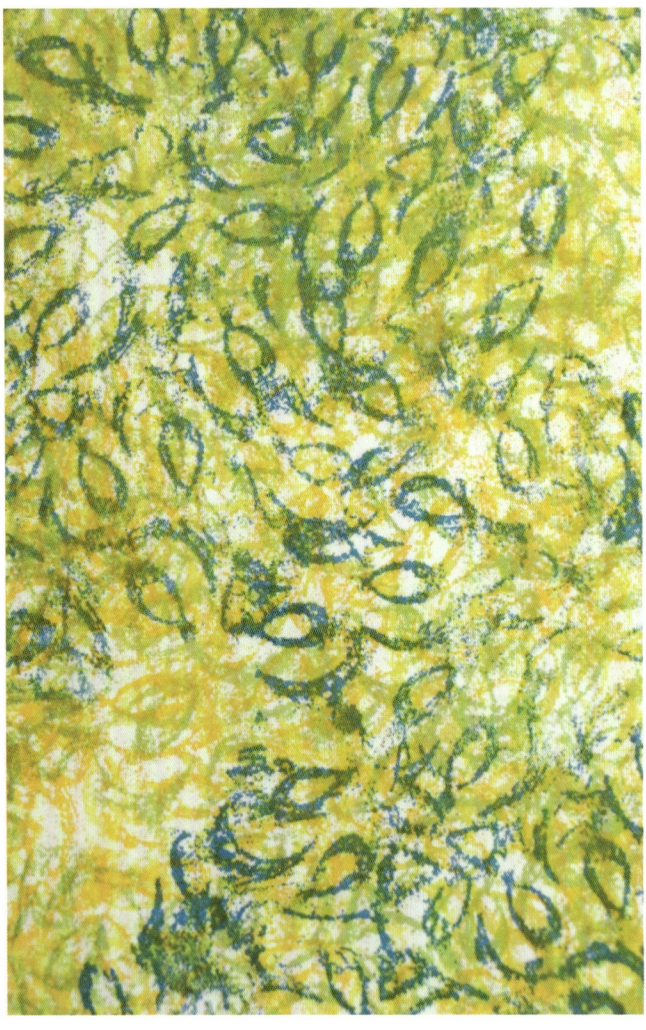

- and then printed with 3 values of scarlet.

Some of the considerations you'll need to make in order to develop the cloth might include:

- the dominance of any individual colour used, and/or the dominance of the secondary colours that have been created. What colour and value is going to be needed to achieve figure-ground, or a doorway into the picture?
- whether the imagery used to create the background needs related imagery to go with it, or something different.
- placement; what kind of balance or movement are you to looking to generate?

If you look at the pictures above and to the right you'll see that Leslie has already started to work compositionally by leaving a void.

3. LINE INTO TEXTURE

This exercise allows you to explore how a simple line design can create texture if heavily over-printed. Choose a line design thermofax and follow these guidelines:

- Pin out your cloth.
- Mix a single colour of thickened dye paint. You can choose to print with one colour, in one value or one colour in several values.
- Print the line design at least three times, all over the cloth, remembering to work off the edges.
- You may need to print as many as six layers; keep looking at what you're achieving, remembering that the purpose of this exercise is to generate background texture by printing with simple line imagery.
- Batch the cloth, rinse it, iron it and then pin it up to consider it.

As a variation or to develop the piece, try the following:

- Print the background using two close or analogous colours instead of a single hue (e.g. yellow and orange, orange and red, blue and purple etc.).
- Print the background using a pale value of a single colour. To move the cloth on compositionally, develop a 'chunkier' version of the line imagery and print it in a much darker value, in the same or a contrasting colour. Think compositionally in terms of placement.
- Develop shape-based imagery and audition it in paper on the piece.

4. LAYERING SCALE

This exercise allows you to explore perspective by layering the same design in three different sizes and three different values. You will need 3 thermofaxes of the same image, in 3 different sizes (small, medium and large).

- Choose your cloth, scour, soda-soak and dry it before pinning it to the print surface.
- Mix a single colour of dye and then adjust it with print paste to achieve three values from dark to light (see page 26 and if you wish, make the value jumps bigger).
- Print the smallest image using the palest value of dye (Pot 1). Work all over the cloth, remembering to print off the edges.
- Now print the middle size image using the medium value dye paint (Pot 2). Work all over the cloth.
- Finish by printing the largest size in the darkest value (Pot 3). At this stage, you may choose not to print all over the cloth. Instead, consider what kind of compositional placement could work.
- Batch, rinse and iron the piece before pinning it up to contemplate your next move.

A simple line design (or sketch) can create fantastic texture if heavily overprinted. Note how one aspect of the image (the centre of the flower) is more dominant

Layering scale with imagery based on an old-fashioned print block

Exercises 5 and 6 can be explored using un-dyed cloth or a pre-dyed cloth in a pale value.

5. USING A SOY WAX RESIST PRIOR TO PRINTING

Using a thermofax to print over a resist created from Soy Wax can be a rewarding experience. Before you start, read the detailed information about using Soy Wax on page 45.

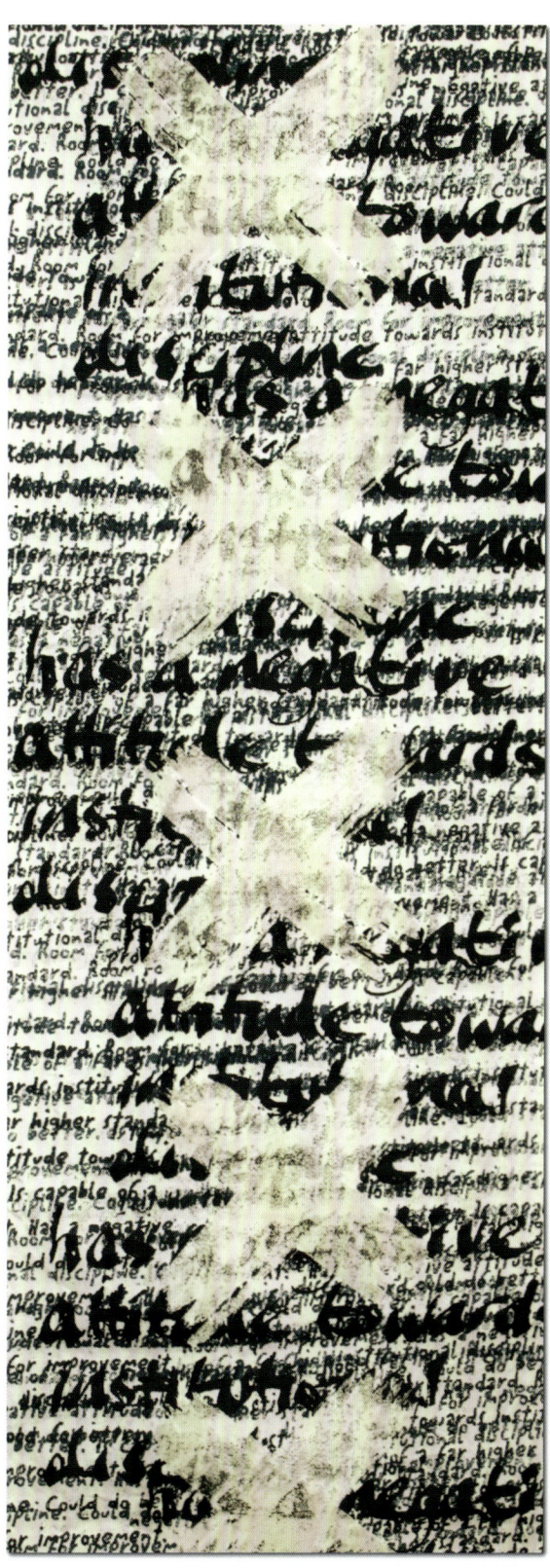

- Place the soda-soaked, dry cloth onto plastic, taping down the four corners to stabilise it.
- Using the tool of your choice (tjanting, bristle or foam brush, cookie cutter, metal stamp etc.), apply the wax. Remember - the wax resist will ultimately be washed out, leaving a strong negative image on the cloth – so think about:
    - placement of the soy wax
    - the imagery used with the soy wax. This could relate to the thermofax image you're going to use, or be something different.
- When the wax has dried, peel the cloth off the plastic and store the plastic.
- Pin the cloth down onto a print bench covered with a dropcloth.

- Using any colour and/or value combination of your choice, print the cloth with your chosen thermofax(es). Make sure you print over the soy wax resist.
- Process the cloth, rinse and make sure you end with hot enough water to remove the soy wax.

In the example shown on the right, we painted the 'X' marks in wax, then over-printed using a small, text-based thermofax, followed by a larger text thermofax up the centre. The cloth was then rinsed. The final red overprinting (see page 22) was achieved in fabric paint using a larger scale version of the second thermofax, which was masked out to restrict the printing to two key words.

Note: You could use washable P.V.A. glue (school glue) as an alternative to soy wax. If so, apply it to the cloth and let it dry completely before proceeding with your printing.

6. PRINTING THROUGH A FREEZER PAPER STENCIL

This project is best explored on cloth where you're seeking to add a compositional element comprised of texture (rather than being solid). As such, you're likely to be working on an existing background in the positive image.

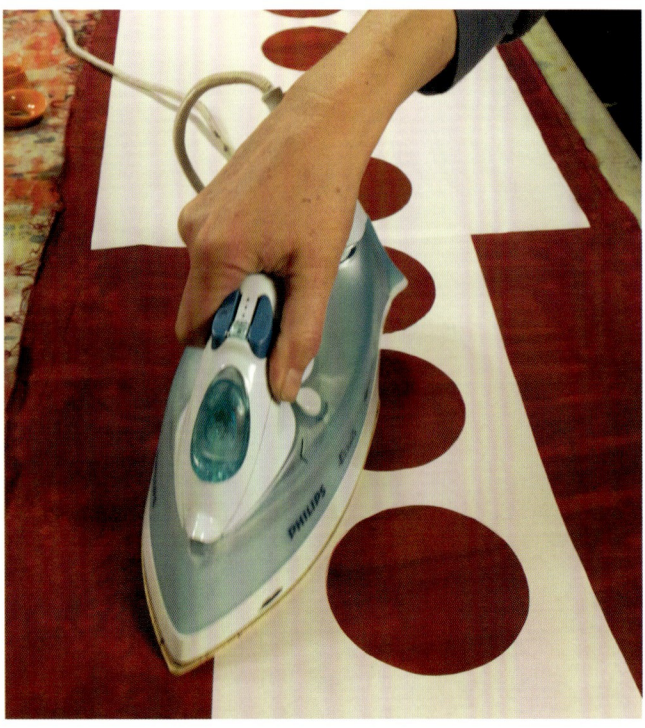

- Cut or tear the stencil from freezer paper.
- Position it onto the cloth and secure with a dry iron. If using soda-soaked cloth, be careful not to scorch any exposed areas.

- Print through the stencil using the thermofax of choice.
- Once the media had dried (or is almost dry), peel off the stencil and process the cloth accordingly.

7. USING FREEZER PAPER RESISTS

Freezer paper is an easy way to create a negative image resist on the cloth. You can cut or tear it into any shape/line you wish before ironing it onto the cloth with a dry iron. If you're planning on printing with thickened dye and therefore have dried, soda-soaked cloth, the soda ash present in the cloth will make scorching more of a potential hazard, so be careful when ironing. Use baking parchment over the stencil/resist if you're worried about scorching.

- Cut or tear out the image(s) you wish to use, to the size you want them.
- Position them on the cloth and secure them by ironing with a dry iron. Be careful not to scorch the cloth.

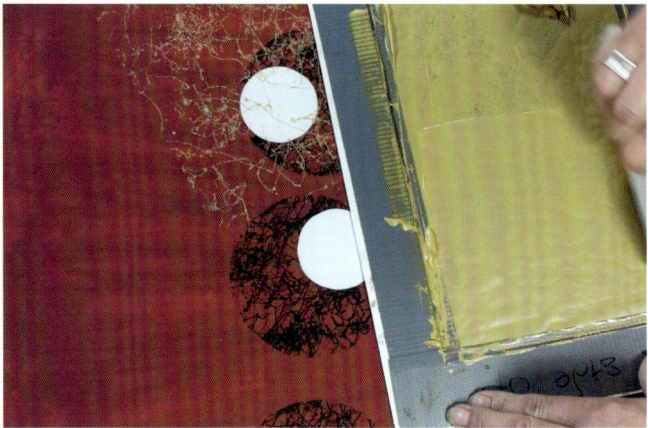

- Using the thermofax of your choice, print over the cloth – right over the freezer paper resists.
- Pay attention to the printing on the edges of the freezer paper resist – sometimes it needs to be a little denser to create a sharp edge.

- When you're finished, peel off the freezer paper and process the cloth accordingly. The freezer paper shapes can be re-used once dry. Store them flat in between sheets of baking parchment.

The photographs show cloth developed with both of these freezer paper approaches. A positive image stencil (a sphere) was applied to the red cloth and then over-printed with black fabric paint. The stencil was then removed and once the paint was dry, a negative shape resist (a smaller sphere) was ironed on to the larger sphere, before over-printing all of the cloth in metallic gold paint, using the same thermofax.

8. EXPLORING TRANSPARENCY & OPACITY

This project encourages you to explore the impact of transparent and opaque fabric paints. Generally speaking and unless otherwise specified on the label, fabric paints are transparent in nature. This can be a beautiful to exploit as underlying colours can either gleam through, or new colours are created with the overlaps when overprinting.

To keep things simple, we've stuck to shades of white and grey for this project, and we suggest you start with a pale value background colour. You do not need to soda soak your cloth when working with fabric paints.

- Pin out a piece of cloth, pre-dyed to a pale value.
- Choose 2 thermofaxes to work with.
- Print with sheer white as the first layer.
- When this first layer is dry, print with a mixture of equal parts sheer and opaque white, using the same thermofax.
- Now put some sheer white into a pot, and add black bit by bit until you get a grey you like.
- To this pot of grey, add an equal amount of transparent extender base – mix well.
- Using the pale grey, print for the third time, using the same thermofax, or switch to your second thermofax.
- Finally (and optional), add a tiny bit of colour (your choice) to the left-over sheer grey, and print a fourth layer with this mixture.
- Let the cloth air-cure overnight, then heat-set.

You could take the cloth to dye processes if you wish to (leave it for 5 days before you do so), or continue printing with fabric paints. Or, you may love the cloth just as it is in which case, leave well alone!

Having explored fabric paints with this simple project, we'd encourage you to take a similar approach using colour.

The piece on the right has been printed with both dye paints and fabric paints.

9. WORKING WITH SHEERS

Printing sheer fabric such as silk organza is a joy as it takes the dye paint so well. Thermofaxes can be great on sheers as they can create a particularly delicate 'tracery' of colour. Sheers are also useful in your repetoire as they can work beautifully on top of other fabrics.

When you print a sheer, it's common for a fair amount of dye paint to go through the sheer, on to the drop cloth. Which means in no time at all your drop cloth can look splendid. Exploit this side-effect by putting silk organza or chiffon on top of another piece of 'good fabric'; this could also be a sheer, or something of a heavier weight. Instead of dye paint being transferred on to your drop cloth, it'll go on to something potentially more worthwhile; resulting in two fabrics being built through one process. The bottom layer may not be perfect, but will often be a good start.

...chara...
f, especially into
bler or more
r face was
by happiness." To
y magic or
lopment.

appearance of, especially into
mething nobler or more
eautiful, her face was

WHAT NEXT?

Having generated background, where you go next is up to you, but do remember to think about the design considerations outlined on page 25. You could choose to continue building the background with your next move, or start to consider the placement of strong compositional elements. Have a dialogue with yourself and the cloth to help you move forward:

- Does the piece have a lot of texture? If so, is it time to consider introducing a shape, strong lines or 'solids'?
- Does the piece contain a lot of line imagery? If so, is it time to consider introducing shape?
- Does the piece have a strong horizontal feel? If so, do you wish to build on this by perhaps introducing a strong horizon line, or would it be worth introducing a vertical element as a contrast?
- Does the piece have a strong vertical feel? If so, do you wish to build on this by perhaps introducing a pathway or strong vertical line, or would it be worth introducing a horizontal element?
- If you've been focused on building background, you may have a strong 'crystallographic' (all over) balance. Do you want to change that and create asymmetry, symmetry or a radial (central point – think Mandala) balance?
- Do you want to create a 'doorway into the picture world' by creating a focal point, pathway (straight, drifting or wiggly?) or horizon line (straight or undulating, low, middle or high?)
- The addition of a new image will drive contrast and visual interest, but if that image is of the same scale, and printed in a close colour and/or value, you'll probably continue to build background, which could be what you want at this stage. Or you could consider sticking to the same image to build relationship, and drive contrast by…
- Manipulating the scale or size of the new or existing imagery (much bigger or much smaller)…
- Printing it in a different colour, or…
- Printing it in a different value: print darker or discharge to create lighter areas, or...
- Printing it in opaque or metallic paint to drive a strong sense of being on top/strongly foreground.

The possibilities are endless, which we acknowledge can be exciting and daunting at the same time. The only way to move forward is to move forward. 'We learn by doing, there is no other way'. And if everything you do isn't satisfactory? Before you consign the piece to the trash and put it down to learning, consider:

- Re-scaling the piece (e.g. fold over the side(s), top and/or bottom). Whilst the whole may not work, a smaller version or a different format might.
- Looking for small 'gems': cut out sections that work and move these on through more wet work or stitch.
- Over-dyeing; chuck the piece into a fairly strong bucket of your choice of colour. If you have no idea what colour to use, try either Black or a Red mixed from 1 part Scarlet (warm red), quarter part Magenta (cold red) and maybe a smidge of Brown.
- Cut it up and use it for quilt making.
- Photograph it and make notes on where you went wrong/why it's not right, then burn it in a ceremonial fashion.

Either way, enjoy your journey and keep learning.

Detail of 'Metamorphosis' by Audrey Critchley, inspired by the City of London

Detail of a stitched thermofax 'sampler' by Claire Higgott

Media & Recipes

PROCION-TYPE MX DYES
The basic list of 'ingredients' for using Mx dyes as paints is;

- Procion-type Mx Dyes
- Sodium Carbonate/Soda Ash. This must be 100% pure and can be sourced from many of the companies listed in the Resources section. We opt to buy ours in bulk from a swimming pool supplies wholesaler.
- Urea (a wetting agent). We buy ours in 25kg sacks from a local Farm/Feed supplier but it's available in small or large quantities from textile suppliers. It must be kept dry to avoid lumping.
- Anti-oxidant; Ludigol or Resist Salt L in the U.K., ProChem Flakes in the U.S.A.
- Water softener; Calgon from the supermarket in the U.K. or U.S.A, or Metaphos from ProChem in the U.S.A.
- Sodium Alginate for making print paste; we use Mantutex RS from Kemtex in the U.K. and ProThick SH from ProChem in the U.S.A.
- A rinsing agent such as Synthrapol or Metapex 38.

Suppliers of these ingredients can be found in the Resources section.

Suitable Cloth for Mx Dyes
Procion-type Mx Dyes are formatted for use with natural fibres such as cotton, linen, hemp, bamboo, silk and viscose/rayon. They will not work on synthetic fibres such as nylon or polyester, nor are they effective with wool – even though wool is a natural fibre. Cellulose fibres will take a dye colour differently to protein fibres. In addition, different fabrics generate a different 'strike' or colour take-up.

Every type of cloth is different; some have fine fibres and others have heavy/thick fibres. Some are tightly woven whilst others have a loose weave structure. Let's take a brief look at this…

Fine vs thick fibres; the Mx dye will react in the fibres once soda ash/sodium carbonate is added to the dye paint or is present in the cloth. Any type of individual fibre is only capable of holding so much dye – a fine fibre will hold less dye and saturate more quickly, a thick fibre will hold more dye and take longer to saturate. Jane Dunnewold suggests imagining the cloth as a car park capable of holding a finite number of cars. When the car park has reached its full capacity, no more cars (dye molecules) will be able to get in – the fibre will be fully saturated. To allow more cars in, you'd have to drive some out through a colour removal or discharge process. So, a very fine Silk Pongee/Habotai is a smaller car park than heavy cotton velvet and less dye will be needed to fill up the silk than the cotton.

Weave structure; a tightly woven fabric will mean that the dye paint has to work harder to get inside the fibres. A loosely woven fabric will be easier for the dyes to penetrate. Imagine different types of fencing; an open trellis will allow the elements through easily whereas a densely woven fence will make it harder for the wind and rain to penetrate. It's the same with a weave structure and what you're working with will have an impact on the crispness and depth of the marks achieved.

The type of cloth you use when thermofax printing will have an impact on the print so it's a good idea to sample first.

Note; we personally avoid using calico/muslin or other 'loomstate' fabrics for anything other than immersion dyeing as it tends to 'push back' the dyes. If you choose to use calico/muslin or loomstate for the projects in this book, scour it very, very well and accept that it will take many processes and perseverance to get a decent depth of colour – but when you do get it, it can be fabulously rich.

As you work with dyes and different fabrics, it's always worth experimenting and making notes on the differences in dye strikes and colours. This means you'll be able to prepare dye paints that are right for the cloth and the colour saturation you're looking for… and you'll waste less dye because your quantities will be more accurate.

Unless you are 100% certain your cloth is 'PFD' (prepared for dyeing), always scour it first. Scouring will remove any dressing or 'size' which would otherwise prevent the dye from reaching the fibre. To scour:

- load the fabric into the washing machine
- add 3 tablespoons of soda ash and 1 teaspoon of Synthrapol
- wash at 60°C

The Role of the Dye
The Mx dyes are your colouring agents (sorry to be obvious!). They're fibre-reactive and Soda Ash is the chemical used to drive the reaction between the dye and the fibre. They're at their most dangerous to health in their dry/powder state so wear a good quality mask when mixing significant quantities. Equally, wear gloves when handling the dyes and if they do get on your skin, don't use bleach to remove them. Instead, use a cleaner such as Reduran to get the worst off - the stains will fade after a couple of days.

Procion-type Mx dyes are classified as 'cold water' dyes but are manufactured to be used between 60-85°F, and will therefore need to be cured or 'batched' to aid striking.

If the dye paint is made without adding soda ash to it, it will last for around 4 weeks if kept cool. Once soda ash is added to the dye paint, the dye will start to bond with the soda – the chemical reaction starts to take place and the paint needs to be used within 4 to 8 hours. This is why we prefer to put the soda ash into the cloth, not the dye paint.

We source our dyes from Kemtex Educational Supplies and the list below shows the names and numbers as used by Kemtex at the time of writing. We've also included the ProChem (a U.S. supplier) equivalents. As a colour range we recommend two sets of basic primaries; 3 cold and 3 warm. Black and Dark Brown have been included to use as colours in their own right or to help you generate complex or dirtied colours and to darken/enrich the primaries (see table overleaf).

Warm Primaries	Cold Primaries
Scarlet Red Mx-3G	Magenta Red Mx-8B
(ProChem Mixing Red 305)	(ProChem Strongest Red 312N)
Royal Blue Mx-R	Bright Turquoise Mx-G
(ProChem Mixing Blue 402c)	(ProChem Turquoise 410)
Golden Yellow Mx-3R	Acid Lemon Mx-8G
(ProChem Golden Yellow 104)	(ProChem Sun Yellow 108)
Kenactive Black K2647 (ProChem Deep Black 609)	
Dark Brown Mx-3G (ProChem Chocolate Brown 511A)	

These eight colours will provide you with endless possibilities but feel free to invest in a larger colour range. It's also worth getting to know one supplier's products as this way, you'll become familiar with how the colours behave.

Many dye manufacturers produce pre-mixed colours that are 'pale' tints of something stronger, e.g. Pale Aqua is often drawn from something like Petrol Green. Think carefully before investing in these pale colours as they are often a poor economy. You can find pale tints by reducing the ratio of dye to print paste. Save your money and invest in colours that can be very difficult to find when you're starting out – such as neutrals.

How much dye to use is a tricky subject - because colour is subjective and different weights and types of cloth will respond differently to the same mixture of dye paint. Another key consideration is that some colours 'strike' faster and more aggressively than others. For example, we find that Magenta (cold red) is the fastest striker, whilst blues tend to be slow. Undertake specific experiments using our recipes as a starting point and adapt them to suit.

The Role of Soda Ash/Sodium Carbonate

Soda Ash or Sodium Carbonate is the chemical fixative needed to generate the chemical reaction with the dyes and fix them into the cloth. Once soda ash is added to a dye paint, the paint must be used within 4 to 8 hours, depending on the climate you're working in.

We prefer to put the Soda Ash into our cloth, rather than our dyes as this means the dye paints will last – if kept cool – for about 4 weeks. We have a soda 'vat' on the go at all times so it's ready when we want to soak cloth. If kept in a lidded bucket, the solution won't evaporate or go off. Wear a mask when mixing significant quantities of soda solution as the fine particles are hazardous if inhaled. This is the recipe we use;

- *3 tablespoons of soda ash per litre of water.*
- We tend to make 10 litres at a time, which requires 450ml/g of soda ash, but 5 litres (which is about half a bucket and requires 225ml/g of soda ash) may be a better quantity for home use. It doesn't go off - just keep it covered so it doesn't evaporate.

Soda Ash doesn't like being dissolved in hot water, so start by putting the required amount of soda ash in a bucket, then add enough tepid water to get it dissolving. Top up with the required amount cold water.

- Put your (dry or very well-spun) cloth in your soda-soaking tub and leave for between 10 and 20 minutes.
- Wring out/spin and work with it wet (more bleed) or wring/spin and line dry to work with it dry (crisper marks).
- If you have a stand-alone spin-dryer, collect the run-off soda solution and re-use it.
- We avoid tumble-drying soda-soaked fabric for several reasons: a residue of soda is left behind on the drum; as the cloth dries, dry particles of soda ash are released into the air and can be inhaled; the effect of heat with soda may damage the cloth. Three good reasons to avoid the tumble dryer.
- Soda-soaked fabric can be stored for later use, but must be bone-dry. Silk will store for about a month whilst cellulose cloth can be kept indefinitely. **Note:** don't store your dry, soda-soaked cloth folded; just stuff it into a bag or a box.

Two soda-soak tubs; clean on the right for white cloth, dirty on the left for dyed cloth

Chemical Water

Chemical Water is the starting point for all dye paints. You can use chemical water that has Urea, a water softener and an anti-oxidant in it, or a simplified version that just has Urea. Let's look at these 3 chemicals/agents;

- **Urea** is a hydroscopic or wetting agent that constantly attracts moisture to itself from the environment. As such, it keeps the dye paints from drying out too quickly. The quantity needed depends on environmental conditions; high humidity will require less Urea and in extreme cases, no Urea. Very dry, arid conditions may require double the amount of Urea specified in our recipe. Please adapt the recipe to suit the conditions you're working in.
- A **water softener** such as Calgon (or Metaphos) is necessary in areas that have very hard water as this can affect the colour strike.
- An **anti-oxidant** such as Ludigol, Resist Salt L or ProChem Flakes is useful where air or water pollution may affect the dye colours.

Whatever combination of ingredients you end up using, chemical water is easy to make and convenient to have ready to hand. Stored cool, it will keep indefinitely and volume quantities are:

Warm Water	Urea	Ludigol	Calgon
5 litres	500ml / 400-500g	25ml	25ml
10 litres	1000ml / 800-900g	50ml	50ml

As a rough guide, 50ml Urea = 35g weighed.
In hot, dry weather, increase the quantity of Urea by approximately 15-20% to prevent the dye paints drying out too quickly.
In humid/damp conditions, reduce the amount of Urea to prevent the dye paints becoming too runny.

Print Paste

A thickening agent - Sodium Alginate - is added to the Chemical Water to make a thick Print Paste. In the UK we use Manutex RS from Kemtex. When working in the U.S.A, we use ProThick SH from ProChem. Dye is added to this paste mixture to create a consistency that's suitable for screen printing and many other direct surface applications.

We usually make about 4 litres at a time and keep it in the fridge, where it will last for about 4 weeks. If you've got some that's been hanging around for longer than this, it may smell of ammonia and have gone off. Dyes can still take well with old paste (although the colour can be less intense), but if you want to be sure, mix a new batch.

However much you make at a time, you can mix by hand, use an old Magimix or better still, a hand-held electric stick blender. We mix a thicker-than-usual print paste that has a 'dropping' rather than a running consistency as it's more suitable for processes such as Breakdown Printing, and is easily thinned by beating more Chemical Water into it. Volume quantities are:

Chemical Water	Sodium Alginate/Manutex RS ProThick SH
1 litre	45ml / 30-35g
2 litres	90ml / 65-70g
4 litres	190ml / 130g

If mixing by hand or with a stick blender, put the required amount of Chemical Water into a tub, start mixing and sprinkle on the Sodium Alginate as you mix.

Mix thoroughly for about 2 minutes and then leave in a cool place for at least 4 hours to thicken up, ideally overnight.

Calgon, Resist Salt L and Urea for making Chemical Water

Beating in the Sodium Alginate with a stick blender

MAKING DYE PAINTS

As mentioned before, we generally prefer to put the soda in the fabric rather than in the dyes. There are several reasons for this;

- The dyes last longer as there's no soda for them to bond with.
- We've observed that thermofaxes can break down more quickly when used with dyes that have soda in them. We suspect this is down to the soda; the repeated pulling of soda-dyes seems to set up an abrasive reaction that breaks down the plastic coating on the mesh.
- Processes such as 'Breakdown Printing' need dyes without soda in them, as the prepared screens will often take all day to dry.

When working with cloth where you want to try to keep a white (or very pale) background, you may want to switch to the soda-in-dye method. It can be hard to keep a white background as it's difficult to avoid staining even with ice-cold rinsing (particularly when Magenta dye is present). Soda-in-dye means that the areas of white cloth you've left un-touched have no soda in them, so staining is less likely.

Different Mx dye colours can strike more quickly and more aggressively than others. We tend to compensate for this when making dye paints by using 'skinny' or 'fat' teaspoons. For example, reds and yellows (and therefore oranges) generally strike more quickly than blues and blacks…

Black; when mixing black, you may want to consider doubling the dye quantity to get a 'true' black. Most blacks can have an undertone, particularly in pale values. Advice is given on how to correct black on page 51.
Turquoise; blues and blacks strike more slowly than yellows, reds or oranges. Turquoise can sometimes be particularly sluggish, so consider increasing the amount of dye by half or using 'fat' measures to help it keep up with faster bed-fellows.
Yellow; when mixing yellow, consider increasing the quantity by half or using a 'fat' measure. Whilst it strikes fairly quickly, yellow is easily contaminated by other colours. You may need to keep larger quantities of yellow as it tends to get used up more quickly because of this.
Magenta; the fastest, most aggressive striker of them all, consider using 'skinny' measures.

How much dye you put into your paint mixture is dependent on you – the more dye, the more intense the colour. Equally, the type of fabric you're using will determine the colour strength; fine silk fibres need less dye than heavier cottons and linens. A good starting point is to mix up a fairly strong mixture and reduce the colour strength as you need to by adding more Print Paste. The following recipe will make a quarter-litre (250ml - about 8 fl oz) of paint. Dyes in our studio are always mixed to this recipe/strength, and weakened with print paste as required.

- *Put a little warm water in a container twice the size of the volume of paint you're making; you'll be stirring vigorously!*
- *Add 2 teaspoons of Mx dye powder and stir well to dissolve.*
- *Now top up to 250ml / 8fl oz with Print Paste.*
- *Beat the mixture well until it's smooth.*

We store our dyes in twist-top ketchup bottles, although these are almost impossible to find now. A good alternative is a clear, polypropalene sauce bottle, which can be obtained from catering suppliers.

Mx dyes will gradually bond with water at warmer temperatures, so their shelf life is limited once mixed. Shelf life can be prolonged by keeping the mixtures in the fridge (covered), but it can be risky to use them after 4 weeks and there's no guarantee on results.

Ultimately, the results depend on dye quantities, fibre types, curing/fixing time and curing temperature (warmer is better!) - you'll need to experiment and/or undertake samples. The more you practise, the more you'll engage with the process and understand it. Ultimately, you'll establish what dye strength is needed to achieve the result you're looking for on the cloth you're using.

Curing/Batching Thickened Dye Paints

In addition to soda ash (which is already in the cloth, or the dye paint), three other 'ingredients' or conditions are required to maximise the dye/fibre reaction:

Moisture:	Almost dry to the touch or very wet
Heat:	15°C - 35°C (60°F - 85°F)
Time:	4 hours as a minimum, overnight or up to 24 hours

This process is often referred to as curing or batching.

Moisture

Dye molecules can penetrate fibre more effectively when moisture is present, although the amount of moisture can be so little that the fabric can feel almost dry to the touch. If the fabric has dried out very quickly or become bone dry to the touch, the reaction may stop, so avoid drying fabric in direct sunlight, drying it too much or too quickly. You can retain moisture content by using plastic sheeting (cover the fabric with it or roll it up). We prefer to let pieces dry off a little before rolling in plastic, as we hate washing plastic! If your cloth does get too dry and you're worried about a good strike, lay it on plastic and re-hydrate it by spraying lightly with Chemical Water. Then roll it up.

Heat

Cure between 15°C - 35°C (60°F - 85°F). If the temperature's too cold, the reaction of the dye is slowed down or even halted completely. To hot and it may dry too quickly for proper curing.

In the summer, or if the studio is heated overnight, let the cloth sit overnight, curing gradually in or under plastic. In winter or in an un-heated studio, roll it up in plastic sheeting (very wet or almost-dry) and slide the tubes in between a folded electric blanket, set to the highest temperature to provide even background heat. If you can't get hold of an old electric blanket, bring the pieces indoors and place them somewhere warm – under (but not on top of) a radiator, over an Aga or near a boiler - and cure for a longer period.

Rolling when wet may cause colours to bleed and blend (which can be fantastic). If you want to keep colours separate, or keep very crisp marks and lines, don't cover or roll when very wet - let the piece semi-dry then cover or roll in plastic before curing.

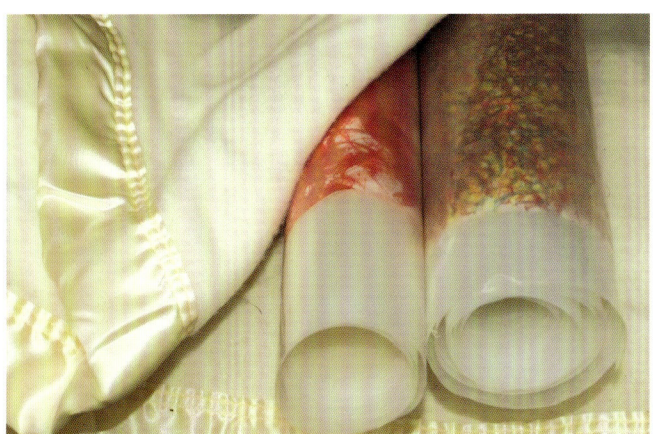

A folded-over electric blanket provides a cheap, even source of heat for curing/batching

Time

Allow 4 hours as a minimum or ideally overnight for curing, as the dye needs time to react with the fibre molecules. Our standard curing time is 12-18 hours/overnight (and we find it exciting to get rinsing the next morning!). If you can't get decent heat for the curing process, let things sit in plastic for 24 hours to give the dyes a better chance to strike.

Rinsing

If you can, use a rinsing agent such as Synthrapol/Metapex 38 as it will 'trap' dye particles and help prevent colour contamination. You'll need a few drops to a half teaspoon when hand-rinsing, and up to 1 teaspoon for a full load when machine washing – it all depends on the size of the load and the heaviness of the fibre. If you don't have a rinsing agent use a mild detergent suitable for delicates or woollens.

- Rinse off excess dye in **cold** water and a rinsing agent in a bucket, changing the water regularly.
- Switch to hand-rinsing with hot water for several changes (be sure to use a rinsing agent when rinsing with hot water).
- Rinse again in cold water.
- Machine wash **cold** with a rinsing agent, once or possibly twice if an aggressive colour (e.g. Magenta) is present.
- Machine wash again in warm water with a rinsing agent at 40-60°C

If you wash in hot water too quickly, excess dye particles may transfer and cause staining (although the use of a rinsing agent will help to prevent this). Remember – the stronger the colours/the more dye you've used, the more washes you'll need. If we know we're taking the cloth on to another dye or discharge process that will subsequently entail more washing, we normally hand-rinse cold, hand-rinse hot, hand-rinse cold, machine rinse cold and then carry on with the next wet process.

Sometimes the sodium alginate/Manutex RS in the thick dye paints can be difficult to remove. This can happen if the dye paint has dried out too fast (e.g. the cloth has been hung to dry in direct sunlight). It rarely happens when printing with a thermofax but if it does, treat the cloth as follows:

- dissolve 1-3 tablespoons of soda in hot (about 60°C) water. The amount of soda is dependent on the amount of cloth, but we find that 3 tablespoons handles a large piece of cloth.
- add a drop of rinsing agent.
- give the piece a good mashing in the bucket, then leave to soak for between 10 and 30 minutes, mashing occasionally.
- rinse out by hand in warm to hot water.
- do a final warm/hot (40-60°C) water rinse by machine.

If the sodium alginate/Manutex RS still hasn't shifted, repeat the process.

Some colours can seem to take forever to rinse out – reds are a good example. If you're worried that you haven't got rid of all excess dye, soak the cloth overnight in cold water, and then rinse it again in the machine at 40°C.

Back-Staining

Back-staining is a method of tinting any white/unprinted areas of cloth with half-exhausted dyes. We're not anti-white but sometimes, a paler tint is more appropriate for the piece. Back-staining can be risky and it'll take some practise to accurately forecast what colour of tint you'll get.

The principle of back-staining is to acknowledge that there may be some semi-active dye present in the cloth after batching. The intention is to use it, with the help of hot water and additional soda-ash to colour any white areas of cloth. To proceed:

- Dissolve 3 tablespoons of soda ash in some warm water in a bucket.
- Half-fill the bucket with hot water (about 60°C – it should feel hot, but not uncomfortable through your gloves).
- Add the printed cloth (do not rinse it first).
- Mash and pound the cloth to help the excess or semi-active dye to release itself into the water.
- Leave the fabric, in this bucket, for at least 30 minutes and up to 4 hours.
- Then rinse the cloth as usual.

When first attempting back-staining, avoid doing it with something you think you're going to love, as there is a risk things could go wrong. The colour of the tint you'll get will depend on the dye colours present in the cloth, and how active they might be. And remember, the fact that individual colours strike at different rates will also have an effect on the resulting tint.

If you're dealing with significant yardage and want to back-stain it, put the fabric into the washing machine and add 3 tablespoons of soda ash. Run the machine on a hot wash (60°C). When the cycle has finished, run the machine again at 40-60°C to get rid of any lingering traces of dye.

DISCHARGE PASTE

Discharge chemicals are used to remove colour from cloth. They won't work on all types of dyed fabrics, so testing is important. Turquoise Mx dye is usually resistant to discharge, so always test any fabric you have containing turquoise.

Mx dyed cloth or commercial discharge cloth is normally discharged with either:

- Jacquard or Dharma Discharge Paste, available ready-mixed
- Formosol powder/crystals
- Thiourea Dioxide (Thiox) powder/crystals

In our studio, we prefer to make our own discharge paste using Formosol. It's much cheaper than buying ready-made paste. Thiox requires an activator in the form of Soda Ash and once mixed has a limited shelf life. Formosol-based paste requires no additional chemicals and will store cool for about 4 weeks.

Formosol Discharge

Formosol will discharge Mx dyed cellulose fibres and silk, but not wool. The powder will oxidise and lose strength when in contact with the air, so decant into smaller tubs as you use it, or pack out the void in the container with bubble wrap or similar.

Formosol is activated by heat and steam and can be mixed with print paste, water or a combination of both to get different consistencies. Always work in a well-ventilated area and/or wear a good quality mask when handling the dry powder/crystals, and when steam ironing.

The basic ratio is 1 part Formosol to 10 parts 'carrying' agent; which can be water or Print Paste. This ratio makes a fairly strong solution, but it's strength can be reduced by adding more water or print paste. To mix 500ml /16fl oz of paste:

- Dissolve 50g (3 generous tablespoons) of Formosol in a little warm (but not hot) water to make a runny paste.
- Top up with 500ml of print paste and beat well with a stick-blender.
- Store covered, in the fridge or somewhere cool.

Note; ProChem sell Formosol in crystal format and it needs to be dissolved overnight in a little water before use. Alternatively, wear a mask and grind the crystals into a powder using a pestle and mortar, or a dedicated old coffee grinder.

Dissolving Formosol into a little warm water before adding print paste

To print and activate Formosol:

- Pin out your dry, coloured cloth (it should not have been soda soaked).
- Print using discharge paste and your chosen thermofax. When you've finished printing, let the cloth dry on the bench, or hang it up.
- When the Formosol paste is completely dry, use a steam iron set to cotton and maximum steam to activate it. The iron is a tool and the way you use it will effect the results you get; the more you steam the more the paste activates. The less you steam the less the paste activates. As such, you can achieve varying shades of discharge by using the iron creatively. Always work in a well-ventilated area and wear a suitable mask.
- Sun activation; you can also experiment by activating the paste with sunlight. Having printed on the paste, hang the piece in direct sunlight; as it dries it will slowly discharge. We've had great results using sunlight and it avoids the fumes. However, do test this approach as generally speaking, the colour and depth of discharge will be different when using sunlight as opposed to a steam iron. We tend not to activate heavier weights of cloth with sunlight as the light tends not to be able to reach deep into the bulk of the fibre.

After activating by steam or sunlight, rinse the cloth by hand or machine. If the dried-in paste proves stubborn to remove, wash in hot water with some soda ash added to it.

Note: Formosol does not have to be mixed with print paste. It can be mixed with water and used for spray-discharge or painting. The ratio is the same; dissolve 50g/3 generous tablespoons of Formosol in a little warm water. Top up to 500ml with cold water. Store in a lidded jar and keep it cool. Formosol-in-water can also be mixed with Formosol paste to create runnier consistencies suitable for needle-nose bottles, painting, and spattering. We usually have Formosol in paste and liquid form ready to use in our studio.

Ready-Made Discharge Paste
Ready-Made discharge paste is a pre-mixed colour removing paste and can be obtained from Dharma Trading and Jacquard. It can be used straight from the tub, which makes it easily accessible, but more expensive. It can be made to go further by mixing it with Print Paste; up to a 50:50 ratio. It's activated by heat and steam. Read the instructions but you may find that you get a better result if you activate it damp (not wet) rather than dry.

Once the applied discharge paste is dry, use a steam iron to activate it

FABRIC PAINTS & ACRYLICS

There are many water-based paints available on the market. Here are a couple of pointers to help you understand the various choices:

- Paints are available ready-mixed in translucent (e.g. see through) colours, opaque colours and metallics.
- All fabric paints are related to acrylic paints. The difference lies in the formula. All paint has a binder, which is the polymer part. The colour comes from the addition of pigment - the pure colour. Fabric paints also tend to have softeners, surfactants (wetting agents) and other ingredients in them to make the paints more sheer and to reduce the impact on the hand of the fabric. This is easily tested; just paint or print a piece of fabric using an acrylic and a good quality fabric paint; nine times out of ten, the acrylic paint will dry to a stiffer hand.
- Most fabric paints (and acrylics) are very light fast, far more so than Mx dyes. The good brands provide data sheets showing the performance of different colours.

A simple way of looking at polymer paint products is to consider two key continuums:

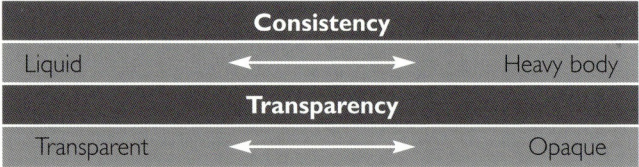

Generally speaking, the C2C studio uses printable consistency, transparent/translucent paints, although metallics veer towards the opaque as the mica that creates the sparkle also creates a level of opacity.

General Information
- Fabric paints are water-based pigment products that coat the surface of the fabric rather than penetrating and reacting with it (as in the case of Procion-type MX dyes). As such, they are suitable for use with both natural and synthetic fibres. Fabric paints have usually had a surfactant added to them to reduce the impact of the paint on the hand of the fabric.
- Textile 'screen inks' are another name for printable fabric paints. They usually contain a drying retardant to reduce the potential of the paint drying in your screen, and sealing the mesh.
- Fabric paints can be bought translucent or opaque and can usually be mixed together to create different levels of translucency (this is usually true when using a single brand, but do test when mixing different brands).
- Metallics can also be mixed with ordinary colours to generate lustrous effects.
- Fabric paint can be made more transparent by mixing with (Transparent) Extender Base. This is the binder the pigment has been suspended in and increasing the amount of base to pigment will increase transparency.
- Most fabric paints require heat to set them. Acrylics aren't designed to be washed, but are okay if heat set.
- Fabric paint will stiffen the hand of the fabric but often, the hand is returned back to normal after washing.
- If you use Mx dyes on cloth subsequent to using fabric paints, the integrity of the paint colour will depend on the opacity of the fabric paint; sheer or transparent colours will be affected the most. It can be very rewarding to use fabric paints (or even a clear medium such as Matte Medium) to act as a permanent resist. Thermofaxes are particularly suitable for this approach as many designs are fine in nature, and don't have much of an impact on the hand of the fabric.

Guidelines on Use
- **Do not** use fabric paints on cloth that has been pre-soaked in soda.
- You can work on ironed or un-ironed fabric; un-ironed can add nice texture, but iron first if this isn't desirable.
- You can work on dry fabric, wet-on-wet or wet-on-damp.
- The paints can be applied through the usual surface application techniques (painting, dragging, stamping, monoprinting etc.) and can be used through a thermofax or silk-screen.
- **NEVER** let paints dry out in any tool; wash up immediately on finishing.
- You can build up layers of fabric paint without heat-setting each layer. Working wet-on-wet can achieve great results but in a similar manner to dye, the true results may not be apparent until the paint has settled into the cloth and is dry.
- On a sunny day, hang the piece in direct sunlight and it'll dry in a jiffy… but never use paints in direct sunlight, as they'll dry out very fast in the thermofax or tool and ruin them.
- One point worth noting is that fabric paint that's stitched and then un-picked will leave holes that won't close (even with washing), which could be a feature – or not.

Heat Setting

It's always a good idea to follow the manufacturers' instructions, but generally speaking, the following principles apply:

- Once the paint has been applied and dried, 'air-cure' for 12-24 hours before heat setting. This will allow the paint to form a more effective bond with the surface of the cloth.
- All fabric paints require heat-setting if they are to be washed, and we always heat set even if the piece is unlikely to be washed. To heat-set, simply iron the cloth using parchment and a dry iron, set to somewhere between the wool and cotton setting.
- Work with the fabric right side up, using a pressing cloth or baking parchment to avoid paint/ink transfer onto the iron and to prevent scorching. Whilst we all hate ironing, don't skimp – follow the manufacturers' instructions on timing and iron settings. We usually flip the cloth over and repeat the process from the back (belt and braces!).

Once the fabric paint has been set, your fabric can be washed, but this isn't a pre-requisite. We don't normally wash until about a week after heat-setting to really allow the paint to settle. Often, any stiffening of the hand of the cloth is returned back to normal after washing.

Acrylics

Acrylic paints were designed for use on paper, board or canvas and are available in a variety of consistencies, all of which can be altered based on what you want to accomplish. Just because the manufacturer didn't envision the paint being used on fabric doesn't mean you can't co-opt it.

As with fabric paints, you get what you pay for. Trying to save money by buying 'school' or 'student quality' acrylics is often a misplaced economy. These lower-grade products generally have less pigment in them and the polymer binders aren't such a high spec. Buy the best quality you can afford. Some great brands include:

- Golden
- Liquitex
- Lascaux
- Tri-Art

All of the colours can be extended with water or added to the vast range of available mediums. They can also be used 'a la prima' (straight out of the bottle/tube), but this will work out expensive and is probably best saved for final accents, or when you've practised!

SOY WAX

Soy Wax is a great resist and a great alternative to traditional Batik wax – generally a mixture of beeswax and paraffin wax. It can be washed out from screens, tools or your cloth with hot water (60°C). Being non-toxic and biodegradable, it won't clog up your pipes or harm the environment. We use a crockpot/slow cooker and a traditional wax pot for melting it in.

Do not mix soya wax and bee or paraffin wax together. If you're going to use a wax pot that's previously had bee or paraffin wax in it, you must get rid of this completely. If not, you'll be back to ironing out the wax and dry-cleaning/ boiling the cloth.

Assemble the following:

- Soy Wax (about 1 kg/2lbs).
- A dedicated pot for melting the wax.
- Tools; distressed bristle brushes, foam brushes, tjantings (Indonesian metal wax 'pens'), metal scrapers, cookie cutters, through a stencil etc.
- A piece of plastic, large enough for the cloth you want to work on, with no creases or wrinkles in it. Alternatively, use a sheet of melamine or similar.
- A roll of kitchen paper/paper towel

Follow these guidelines:

- Make sure the wax is fully melted and hot to ensure good results. Soy wax is very versatile as it cools more slowly than other wax types but still dries quickly.
- Place the tool you're going to be using in the hot wax, and let it heat up.
- Apply the wax to your cloth in any manner of choice. We find it's helpful to tamp off excess wax from the tool on to a folded piece of paper towel before working on the cloth.
- Remember, the wax is the resist and therefore the design will be in the *negative* image once you've over-printed it with the thermofax.
- Let the wax dry (which won't take long – about 1 minute).
- Remove the cloth from the plastic and pin it onto the print bench, on top of a dropcloth.
- You're now ready to overprint with your thermofax.
- Process and rinse the cloth according to the media you've used.
- Remember that the soy wax will wash out at 60°C.

Colour Mixing

Colour is very subjective; one person's burgundy is another person's plum. As such, the colour recipes provided in this section are to our personal descriptions, and may not match what you see in your head. If so, re-label them in a way that makes sense to you. What we discuss is relevant whether you're using thickened dye paints or fabric paints – although with fabric paints, you have the option of using white, which makes mixing neutrals much easier.

The results you'll get when mixing cold colours together vs warm colours will be quite different. For example;

Cold mixes;
- Lemon Yellow & Magenta will give you a bright, brilliant, 'acid' orange.
- Lemon Yellow and Turquoise will make a brilliant, sparky emerald green.
- Turquoise & Magenta will give you a bright, sparky purple.

Warm mixes;
- Golden Yellow & Scarlet will give you a warm, rich orange.
- Golden Yellow & Royal Blue will give you a dirty green… not quite olive, but almost.
- Royal Blue & Scarlet will give you a plummy purple.

Mixing Proportions
Ultimately, the best way to learn about colour and colour mixing is to get stuck in with the paints. The first rule of thumb is never assume that the way a colour looks in the pot or when wet on the fabric is the way it'll look once rinsed and dried. This is a tricky thing for your eyes and your head to manage, but will come with practice and observation. As you work, consider making a record on paper with a note of the colours used, in what proportions and combinations. Equally, tear off little bits of cloth from your experiments and glue them into a reference book as this will give you a truer record of the way the different mixtures work on cloth.

When mixing, you'll get different results depending on the proportion of colours used, for example;

- A mix of Lemon Yellow & Magenta where the proportion of yellow is greater than Magenta will give you a bright Yellow-Orange.
- A mix of Lemon Yellow & Turquoise where the proportion of yellow is greater than Turquoise will give you a bright lime – or yellowy – green.
- A mix of Turquoise and Magenta where the proportion of turquoise is greater than magenta will give you a bright blue-violet.
- A mix of Golden Yellow and Scarlet where the proportion of scarlet is more than the golden yellow will give you a warm, red-orange.

and so on.

So, you need to think about what colours you're trying to achieve. Are you looking for cold, bright, high-energy colours? If so, explore the cold primaries. Are you looking for rich, muted, warm colours? If so, explore the warm primaries. Then try mixing cold colours with warm colours to find out what else you can achieve.

We've done some mixing to give you a starting point, but do remember that dyes from different manufacturers will vary, so don't expect your colours to be identical to ours (and it's always hard to show true colours in a photograph). All of the colours shown in this section were made a follows:

- all key colours were mixed using the basic dye paint recipe on page 40.
- the mixtures were stirred together in pots and then scraped on to soda-soaked cotton sateen with a credit card. It's worth noting the way the colour is applied will make a difference to the end result, as some methods will drive more dye into the fibre, and others less.
- the fabric was then batched overnight and rinsed.

Here, thermofax printing has provided a great background for embroidery (Pat Deacon)

Going Green
We started by experimenting with different types of Green:

1. 10 parts Acid Lemon, 1 part Turquoise
2. 10 parts Golden Yellow, 1 part Turquoise
3. 1 & 2 mixed together
4. 10 parts Turquoise, 1 part Acid Lemon
5. 10 parts Turquoise, 1 part Golden Yellow
6. 4 & 5 mixed together
7. 10 Parts Acid Lemon, 1 part Royal Blue
8. 10 parts Golden Yellow, 1 part Royal Blue
9. 7 & 8 mixed together
10. 1 part Acid Lemon, 1 part Royal Blue
11. 1 part Golden Yellow, 1 part Royal Blue
12. 1 part Acid Lemon, 1 part Turquoise
13. 1 part Golden Yellow, 1 part Turquoise

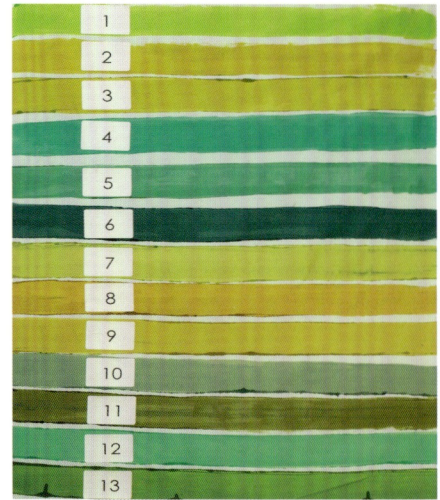

The Blues
And then we moved on to explore the blues..., and used Black and Dark Brown to enrichen or dirty the blues:

1. 10 parts Royal Blue, 1 part Black
2. 10 parts Turquoise, 1 part Black
3. Equal parts Royal Blue and Black
4. Equal parts Turquoise and Black
5. 2 parts Royal, 2 parts Black and 2 parts Print Paste
6. 2 parts Turquoise, 2 parts Black and 2 parts Print Paste
7. Equal parts Royal Blue and Turquoise
8. 2 parts Royal Blue and 1 part Dark Brown
9. 2 parts Turquoise and 1 part Dark Brown

...and remember, you can add print paste to any of these recipes to achieve paler values

Using Black & Brown to Enrichen
We use Black & Brown as agents for generating rich colour effects. We use Black as the darkening (or dirtying) agent for blues and reds and Brown as the darkening agent for yellows and reds. We make this decision based on Kenactive Black dye having a blue-green undertone. If it's used with the yellows, you'll get greens - great greens but certainly not ochre! If it's used to darken magenta you'll get a pinkish maroon whilst if you darken magenta with brown you will get a deep, rich red. The photograph will show you the different kinds of reds you can achieve using Black and Dark Brown to enrichen, and here's how we did them.

Rich Reds
1. 2 parts Magenta, 1 part Black
2. 2 parts Scarlet, 1 part Black
3. 1 & 2 mixed together
4. 2 parts Magenta, 1 part Dark Brown
5. 2 parts Scarlet, 1 part Dark Brown
6. 4 & 5 mixed together
7. 2 parts Magenta, 1 part Scarlet, 1 part Dark Brown
8. 2 parts Scarlet, 1 part Magenta, 1 part Dark Brown
9. 2 parts Scarlet, 1 part Dark Brown, 1 part Black
10. 2 parts Magenta, 1 part Dark Brown, 1 part Black.

Complex Colours

We define a complex colour as a colour that's been adulterated to make a 'dirtier' version of itself. The key principle is to adulterate the colour by adding a smidge of its complementary colour. The complementary 'couplings' are:

Primary Colour	Complementary
Red	→ Green
Yellow	→ Purple
Blue	→ Orange
Secondary Colour	**Complementary**
Green	→ Red
Purple	→ Yellow
Orange	→ Blue

When mixing any complex colour, the end result is always subjective to the proportions you use, for example;

- To mix a complex secondary, start by mixing equal parts of the two primaries required and then add up to a half-part of the complementary colour, bit by bit, until you get the colour you're seeking.

For example, to mix ochre;

- start with Golden Yellow (warm yellow). Bit by bit, add purple until the golden yellow had turned to the ochre you see in your head.
- as you have two reds (warm and cold) and two blues (warm and cold) in your colour palette to make that Purple, there's room to find plenty of ochre. You could also choose to use Brown as the dirtying agent, so try different approaches.

So, we did some colour sampling with Complex colours and you'll find the recipes that correspond with the images below.

Ochre/Sand

1. 10 parts Golden Yellow, 1 part Dark Brown
2. 10 parts Golden Yellow, 2 parts Dark Brown
3. 10 parts Lemon Yellow, 1 part Dark Brown
4. 10 parts Golden Yellow, 1 part Scarlet, 1 part Royal
5. Mix No. 4, and then add an equal amount of print paste to reduce the value.
6. Now take mixture No.5, and add an equal amount of print paste to reduce the value even further.
7. Take mixture No.6, and add an equal amount of print paste to achieve a very pale tint.

Rust Orange/Brown

1. 4 parts Golden Yellow, 2 parts Scarlet, 1 part Royal Blue
2. 2 parts Golden Yellow, 2 parts Scarlet, 1 part Turquoise
3. 4 parts Acid Lemon, 2 parts Scarlet, 1 part Royal Blue
4. 2 parts Acid Lemon, 2 parts Scarlet, 1 part Royal Blue
5. 4 parts Golden Yellow, 2 parts Magenta, 1 part Royal Blue
6. 4 parts Golden Yellow, 2 parts Magenta, 1 part Royal Blue, 1 part Black

Trying different approaches will produce a never-ending range of complex colours and that's the magic of it all! Here are a couple more suggestions to play with based on the Mx dye paint colours mentioned earlier;

- *Olive Green;* mix equal parts Warm Yellow and Warm Blue and then add (up to a half part) of Cold Red (Magenta) or Warm Red (Scarlet). Or, add Black bit by bit to Warm Yellow. You'll get a different dirty green by using a cold yellow instead of golden yellow.
- *Petrol Green;* 1 part Cold Blue (Turquoise), a smidge of Black and a smidge of Cold Yellow (Acid Lemon). Experiment with your 'smidge' amounts.

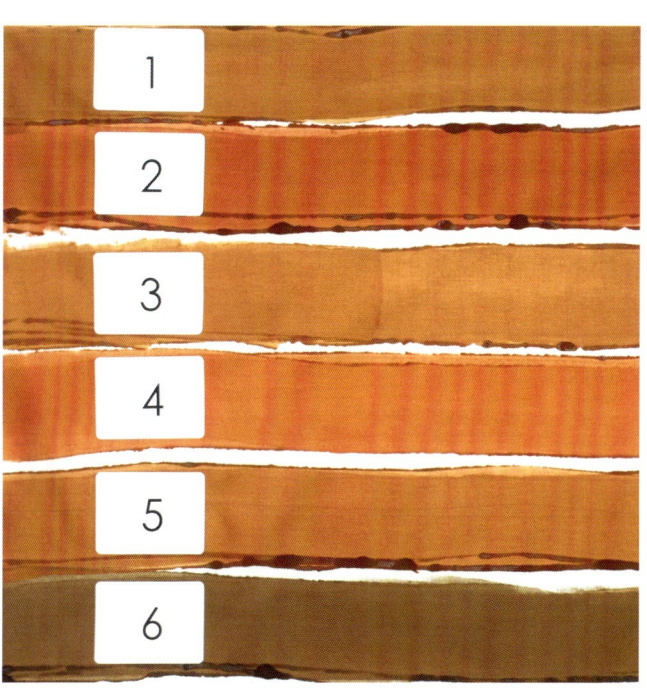

Neutrals & Muddy Colours

Mixing neutrals and muddy colours can be intimidating as essentially, you'll need to mix all 3 primaries, and then add significant amounts of print paste to get pale values. We did some experiments using Dark Brown and Black as our base colours, adding print paste and then progressively adding different colours to this base mixture.

The photographs should show that the black-based neutrals have a slight green tinge to them, as the black we use has a bias towards a bluey-green.

Note; if at any time the value gets too dark, simply add more print paste.

Neutrals based on Brown:
1. 1 part Dark Brown to 10 parts Print Paste
2. To mixture 1, add 1 part Golden Yellow
3. To mixture 2, add 1 part Scarlet
4. To mixture 3, add 1 part Green (and experiment with different Greens!)
5. To mixture 4, add 1 part Golden Yellow
6. To mixture 5, add 1 part Royal Blue
7. To mixture 6, add 1 part Scarlet

Neutrals based on Black:
1. 1 part Black, 10 parts Print Paste
2. To mixture 1, add 1 part Golden Yellow
3. To mixture 2, add 1 part Scarlet
4. To mixture 3, add 1 part Green (and as before, experiment with the type of Green you use)
5. To mixture 4, add 1 part Golden Yellow
6. To mixture 5, add 1 part Royal Blue
7. To mixture 6, add 1 part Scarlet
8. Take half of mixture 7 and add an equal amount of print paste to reduce the value.

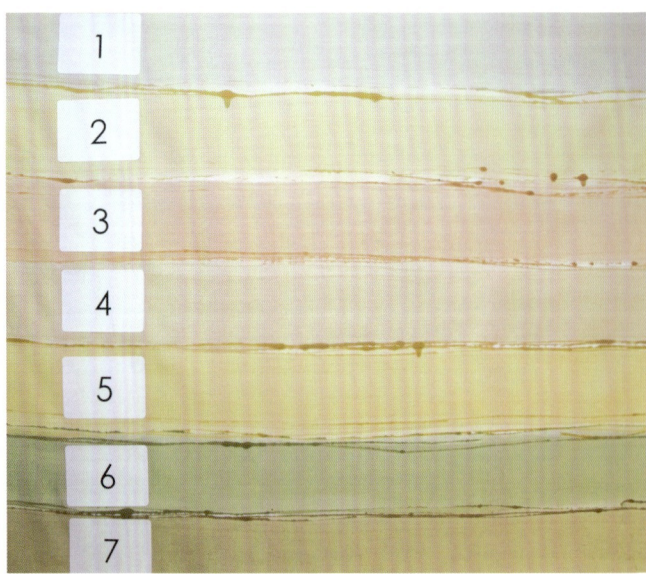

Neutrals based on Brown

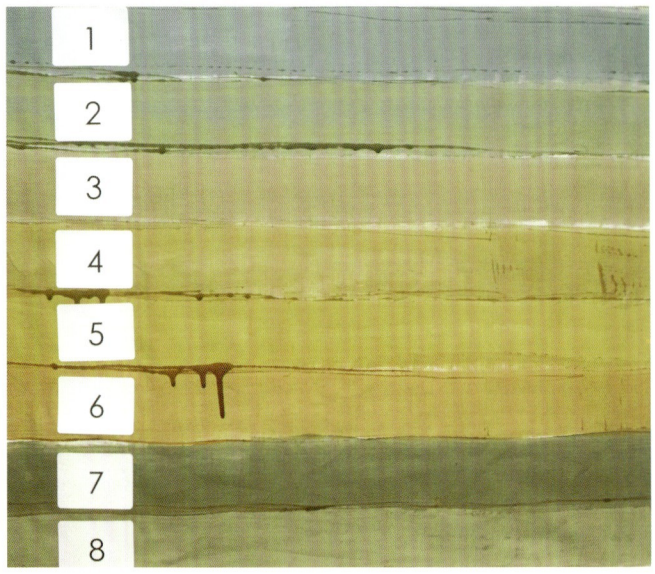

Neutrals based on Black

Great neutrals can be achieved through discharge. 'Wisley Revisited' by Audrey Critchley

Correcting Black... and finding Grey

Finding Black or Grey when using fabric paints is easy; the black is a true black and grey can be found by adding black paint to white paint, bit by bit. With dyes, we have no white dye with which to achieve grey and most black dyes have a bias towards another colour. This bias can normally be established when mixing the 'black' in a weak strength as it often reveals its true colour bias. For example Kenactive Black tints down to a blue-green, not a grey.

The principles of achieving True Black are the same as any other colour mixing approach; you need to get the correct proportions of all three primary colours – to the point they cancel each other out and create black. Try the following:

1. establish the bias of the black dye you have
2. add the complementary colour of the bias shade until you cancel it out, but no more. Do this bit by bit, checking the colour as you progress.

For example:

- black that has a bias towards blue; add orange or rust orange
- black that has a bias towards red; add green or olive green
- black that has a bias towards purple; add yellow, or ochre

We know that Kenactive Black (from Kemtex in the U.K.) has a blue-green bias, so try the following approaches to find black and grey:

- 1 part each of Kenactive Black and Dark Brown dyes: this can often work well on silk, but doesn't generate True Black or Grey on cotton.
- This recipe seems to perform well on cotton and silk:

    - 1 part Kenactive Black
    - 1/4 part Rust Orange
    - 1/4 part Red Brown

You can now add print paste to start taking this black mix down to grey.

We could have spent many more hours, days or weeks exploring colour, and this underlines that to understand colour, you have to play with it. The permutations are infinite and fiddling with the proportions is one of life's great joys! Ultimately it's important to remember that we all see and describe colours differently. The kind of terracotta, olive, aubergine, ruby, chestnut, ochre, rust orange, plum that you're seeking will be different to someone else's. As such, you need to experiment with proportions until you get the colour you want. Having got it – make a note of how you got it or commit it to memory. Or just have fun trying to find it again!

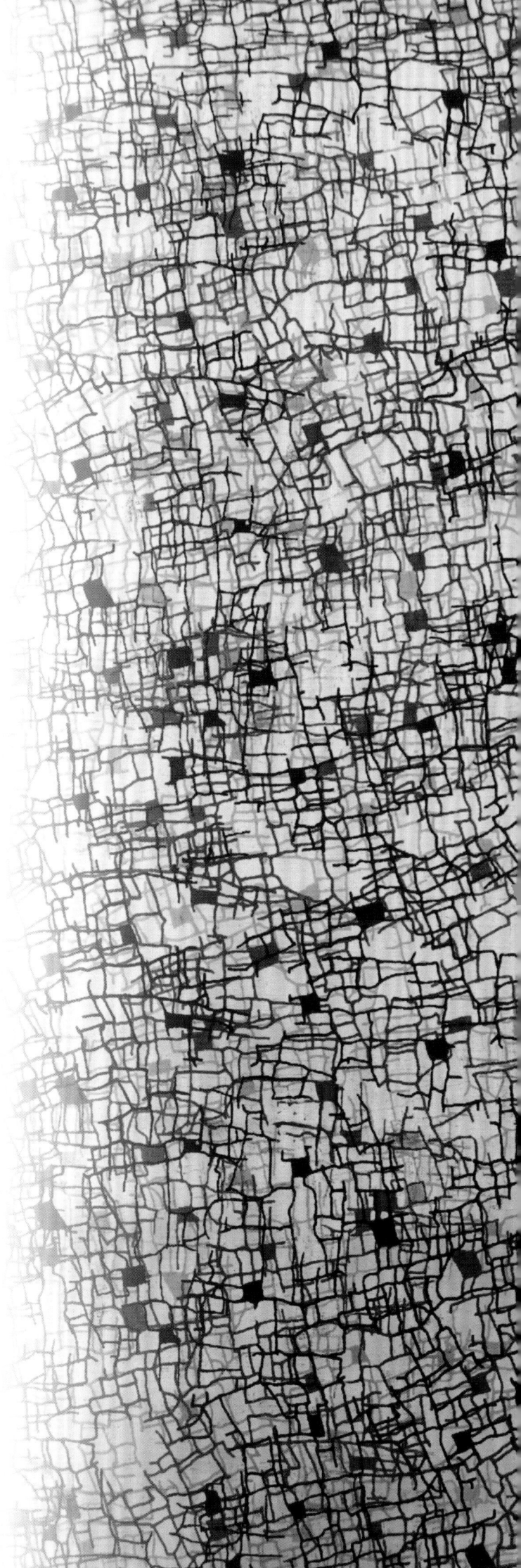

Line into texture using white, grey and black
(Claire Higgott)

Resources/Suppliers

This first section provides information on suppliers who will burn thermofax screens from your own imagery. Some also have a selection of ready-made screens to choose from. It is also worth googling 'thermofax' and seeing what you find!

Europe
Claire Higgott of Thermofax Screens;
www.theromfaxscreens.co.uk
Ruth Brown of Stone Creek Silk;
www.stonecreeksilk.co.uk
Guenther Panenka of PDPM; www.pdpm.de

USA
Su Butler; www.subudesigns.com
Pam Relitz; rockitz@tds.net
Marcy Tilton: www.marcytilton.com
Bobby Vance; fiberartBV@aol.com
Northwoods Studio; www.northwoodstudio.us
Lyric Kinard; www.lyrickinard.com
Sonja; www.friendsfabricart.com
Jeanne Surber & Andi Perejda; www.jandidesigns.com

Canada
Susan Purney Mark; patchworkstudio@shaw.ca

Australia
Nehoc Australia Pty. Ltd: www.nehoc.com.au

In terms of general supplies, dyes, paints, chemicals and tools, the web site (www.committedtocloth.com) has a list of suppliers, but the following companies will be able to provide you with what you need. Remember, if it's a web-based company, many ship worldwide.

EUROPE

Art Van Go
The Studios, 1 Stevenage Road, Knebworth, Herts G3 6AN
www.artvango.co.uk

Atlantis Art
7-9 Plumber's Road, London E1 1EQ
www.atlantisart.co.uk

Bramble Patch (The)
West Street, Weedon, Northamptonshire NN7 4QU
www.thebramblepatch.co.uk

Fibrecrafts/George Weil
Old Portsmouth Road, Peasmarsh, Guildford, Surrey GU3 1LZ
www.fibrecrafts.co.uk

Great Art (web-based)
www.greatart.co.uk

Jacksons Art Supplies
Arch 66, Station Approach, Fulham, London SW6 3U
1 Farleigh Place, London N16 7SX
www.jacksonsart.co.uk

Nannas Verksted
Skoleblakken 29, 1628 Engelsviken, Norway
www.nannasverksted.no

Quilt und Textile
Sebastiansplatz 4, Munich 80331, Germany
www.quiltundtextilkunst.de

Patchwork Shop
www.patchworhshop.de or www.pdpm.de

Spektrum Textil
Radhusvej 2, 2920 Charlottenlund, Copenhagen, Denmark
www.spektrumtextil.dk

Thermofax Screens
Foxley Farm, Foxley, Towcester NN12 8HP
www.thermofaxscreens.co.uk

Whaleys
Harris Court, Great Horton, Bradford, West Yorkshire
www.whaleys-bradford.ltd.uk

Winifred Cottage
17 Elms Road, Fleet, Hampshire GU51 3EG
www.winifredcottage.co.uk

Zijdelings
Kapelstraat 93a, 5046 CL Tilberg, The Netherlands
www.zijdelings.com

NORTH AMERICA

Art Cloth Studios (U.S.A.)
www.artclothstudios.com

Dick Blick (U.S.A.)
PO Box 1267, Galesburgh, IL 61402
www.dickblick.com

Dharma Trading Company (U.S.A.)
1604 Fourth Street, San Rafael, California 94901
www.dharmatrading.com

GS Dye (Canada)
250 Dundas Street West, No. 8, Toronto M5T 2Z5, Ontario
www.gsdye.com

Jerry's Artarama (U.S.A.)
www.jerrysartarama.com

Maiwa (Canada)
6-1666 Johnston Street, Granville Island, Vancouver V6H 3SZ, B.C.
Maiwa.com

ProChemical & Dye (U.S.A.)
PO Box 14, Somerset, MA 02726
www.prochemical.com

Rupert, Gibbon & Spider (U.S.A.)
PO Box 452, Healdsburg, CA 95448
www.jacquardproducts.com

The Art Store (U.S.A.)
801 73rd Street, Windsor Heights, IA 5-312
www.shoptheartstore.com

NEW ZEALAND & AUSTRALIA

Artbeat of Tasmania (Tasmania, Australia)
85 Channel Highway, Kingston, Tasmania 7050
www.artbeattas.com

Artisan Books (Australia)
159 Gertrude Street, Fitzroy 3065, Victoria
www.artisan.com.au

Batik Oetoro (Australia)
8/9 Arnhem Close, Gateshead, NSW 2290
www.dyeman.com

Essential Textile Art (Australia)
PO Box 3416, Rundle Mall, SA 5000
www.essentialtextileart.com

KraftKolour (Australia)
Box 379, Whittlesea, Victoria 3757
www.kraftkolour.com.au

New Zealand Quilter (New Zealand)
PO Box 14567, Kilbirnie, Wellington 6241
www.nzquilter.co.nz

The Thread Studio (Australia)
6 Smith Street, Perth 6000
www.thethreadstudio.com

Further Reading

Surface Design

Many books are available on surface design and the use of different media, including the following:

Holly Brackman: The Surface Designers' Handbook, Interweave Press, 2006
Jane Dunnewold (Complex Cloth Resources): Jane has several DVD's and 'books on CD', so be sure to check out her website for the full list of titles, www.artclothstudios.com
Jane Dunnewold: Art Cloth; a guide to surface design for fabric, Interweave Press 2010
Rayna Gilman: Create your own hand-printed cloth, C&T Publishing, 2008
Ruth Issett; Colour on Paper & Fabric, Batsford 1998
Sherrill Kahn: Creating with Paint, Martingale & Company, 2001
Joanna Kinnersly-Taylor: Dyeing & screen printing on textiles, A&C Black, 2003
Ann Johnston: Color by Accident (1997) and Color by Design (2001), self published
Jean Ray Laury: Imagery on Fabric, C&T Publishing, 1992
Rheni Tauchid: The New Acrylics, Watson-Guptill, 2005
Kate Wells: Fabric Dyeing & Printing, Conran Octopus, 1997

Other books by Committed to Cloth

Our stable of books (some co-authored with Jane Dunnewold) is building – check out the titles on the opposite page. Order direct from www.committedtocloth.com or find a distributor in the Resources section of the website.

Detail of 'Rost' (Rust) by Claudia Helmer